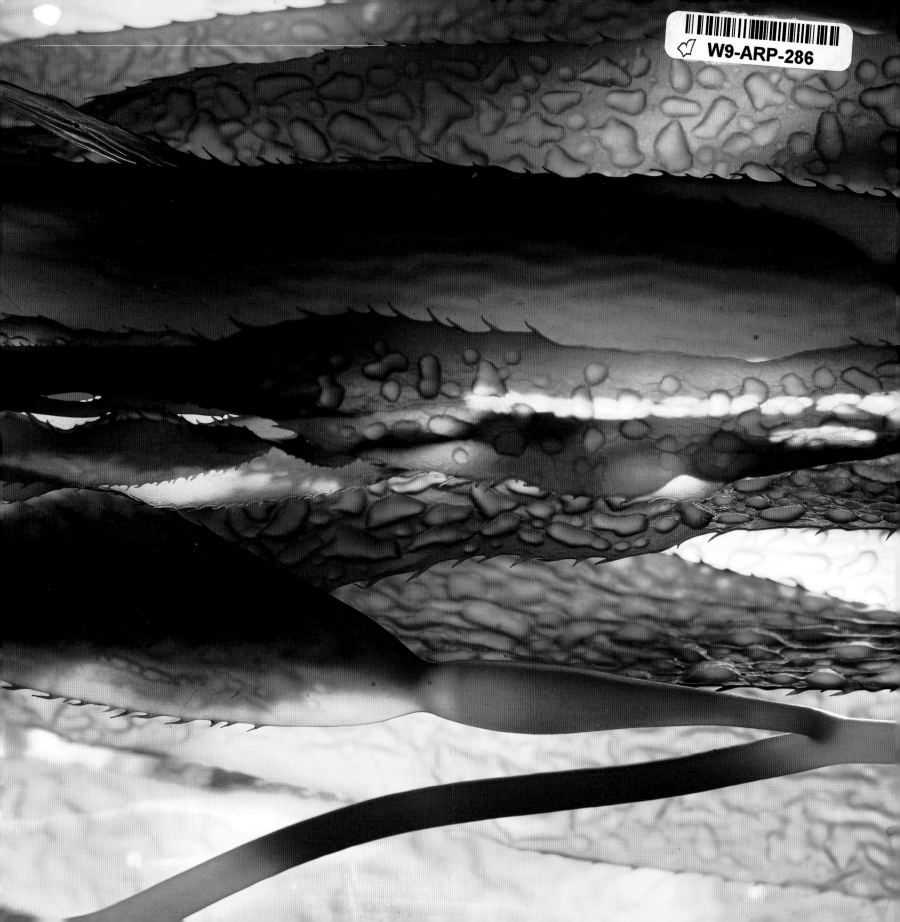

To Raydean From Kenny 1-13-95

# SEAFOOD ON THE GRILL

## SIMPLE AND SAVORY RECIPES FOR FISH AND SHELLFISH

BY
DAVID BARICH AND THOMAS INGALLS

PHOTOGRAPHY BY
DEBORAH JONES

FOOD STYLING BY
SANDRA COOK

HarperPerennial

*A Division of* HarperCollins*Publishers*

*We would like to thank the following retailers, galleries, and individuals, all of whom helped in many ways to make this book look the way it does.*

Fillamento, Sue Fisher King, Zonal, Anita del Castro, Missy Hamilton, Buddy Rhodes, Kathleen Kelly, Jeri Jones, Michel Rabaste, Helga Sigvaldadottir, Liz Zivic, Vicki Roberts-Russell, Inge Hoogerhuis, and Bob and all the guys at Mission Market Fish & Poultry

A special note of thanks to Carolyn Miller for all her ideas, help, and suggestions.

For information, write:
HarperCollins Publishers, Inc.
10 East 53rd Street
New York, NY 10022

Printed in Hong Kong.

Grateful acknowledgment is made to Penguin Books for permission to reprint copyrighted material from *Traveling Light* by Bill Barich (New York, 1985).

FIRST EDITION

Produced by David Barich.
Book and Cover Design: Ingalls + Associates
Designers: Tom Ingalls, Tracy Dean, and
   Margot Scaccabarrozzi
Photography and Set Design: Deborah Jones
Food Stylist: Sandra Cook
Prop Stylist: Sara Slavin

**Library of Congress Cataloging-in-Publication Data**

Barich, David.
      Seafood on the grill / by David Barich
   and Thomas Ingalls. — 1st ed.
            p.         cm.
      Includes bibliographical references
   and index.
      ISBN 0-06-096984-9 (pbk.)
      1. Barbecue cookery.   2. Cookery
   (Seafood).   I. Ingalls, Thomas.
   II. Title.
   TX840.B3B36   1993
   641.5′784—dc20                    92-54251
                                         CIP

93 94 95 96 10 9 8 7 6 5 4 3 2 1

My casting fell into the hypnotic rhythm I'd been after at Hat Creek, obliterating consciousness, and I had one of those rare moments of epiphany that come when you're entirely open to them. I lost any sense of the McCloud as a specific river. It began to recapitulate every other river I'd fished, to exist briefly as an absolute form. The water stopped being merely water and became instead an adjunct of my body, so that I was joined to it in a steady flow. The moment didn't last very long, but that was all right. That was fine.

Bill Barich
"Hat Creek and the McCloud"
from *Traveling Light*

# CONTENTS

# INTRODUCTION

Fish is an almost perfect food. Low in fat and high in protein, fast and easy to cook, full of flavor and easily digestible, it is limited only by its perishability and lack of availability. Now, thanks to the growing practice of fish farming and improved marketing systems, both shellfish and fish of all kinds are becoming more and more available around the country.

More than any other food, grilled fish seems to typify the way we eat now. Grilling is a favorite method of cooking fish because it is so quick and so simple, and because it brings out the flavor of fish without adding fats and calories by coating fish with batter or bread crumbs, or by frying it. Most fish for the grill benefit from a brief marinade in a small amount of oil and a few flavoring ingredients; mesquite and aromatic woods add their own subtle perfume. Grilling fish quickly over a hot or medium-hot fire gives it a seared, grid-marked exterior that contrasts beautifully with the tender interior flesh. And grilled fish is perfectly complemented by any of a number of fresh, quickly made sauces, like the ones you will find in these pages.

The recipes in *Seafood on the Grill* are quick, simple, and light. We've used lots of fresh vegetables and fruits, and have tried to keep most of the recipes low in fat. When we do use mayonnaises or butter sauces, we do so with an easier conscience because of the low fat content of fish. Because the fat in fish is either unsaturated or poly-unsaturated, unlike the fat in red meat, we feel fine about eating oily fish such as salmon and tuna, especially now that many scientists believe that the omega-3 oil found in these fish actually reduces cholesterol.

Most of our recipes serve four people and can be easily multiplied for larger get-togethers. Because fish cooks so quickly, we've added at least one other grilled food to each list of suggested accompaniments in order to make full use of the lighted coals. *Please note:* In some cases, instructions for cooking one or more side dishes are included in the main-course recipe. We've tried to be as specific as possible about the other suggested accompaniments, to make it easier for you to create them. You will find complete recipes for some of these side dishes in three of our other grill books: *Grill Book, The Art of Grilling,* and *Vegetables on the Grill.*

Our recipes call for fish to be marinated at room temperature while the coals are heating, and most of the side dishes can be cooked and all of the grilled dishes can be prepared for grilling during this time period. Generally we try to pair fairly mild flavors with mild-tasting fish and more robust flavors with fish that are more assertive in taste, but we also encourage you to use any of the marinades and sauces that sound appealing with any fish you like. It's hard to go wrong with good, fresh ingredients and fish hot off the grill. You also might want to try some of the marinades and sauces used on poultry, meat, vegetables, and fish in our other grill books, including *Chicken on the Grill.*

Chapter 1 of *Seafood on the Grill* discusses different kinds of grill and grilling techniques. The most helpful tools for grilling fish are discussed at the end of this chapter. Please read "Know Your Fire," on page 16, to learn the different stages of heat. We prefer to grill most fish over a hot fire, especially when grilling on a kettle grill, which is fixed at 6 inches from the coals. There are some exceptions to this general rule, however, and the degree of heat you use is important to cooking fish successfully.

Chapter 2 begins with a glossary of fish and shellfish, which includes suggestions on how to grill the various types and which fish can be substituted for them. "Secrets of the Grill: A Little Guide to Grilling Fish and Shellfish," on pages 35–36 of this chapter, is a summary of our best tips for grilling fish successfully. It's followed by a glossary of special ingredients to help you find and use any unfamiliar spices, sauces, and so on.

Perfecting your skills at grilling fish and finding your favorite recipes is a happy way to add variety to your cooking. In many ways, fish is an ideal food because it appeals to us on such a basic level: It brings back memories of times spent by the water—trout fishing in the mountains, boat fishing in northern lakes, picnics on the beach. And the memory may go back even farther, to some Edenic climate and time when the fruits of the water and the land were easily found and gathered. We believe that grilling fish outside in mild weather, then serving it with a good sauce and the right side dishes and beverage, is a little bit of paradise. We've tried to create twenty-five of the best grilled-fish meals for this book, along with tips for grilling moist, flavorful fish, to help you find a small corner of the garden wherever your grill may be.

# Tools, Fire, and Smoke

Fish can be cooked on just about any kind of grill, from a cooking rack over a campfire to the most elaborate gas grill. Our discussion of grills is divided between those fueled by charcoal and those that run on gas. We prefer charcoal grills for cooking fish, as we think mesquite or other hardwood charcoal is an important flavor enhancer for the mild taste of fish. At the same time, we understand the advantage of cooking fish on a gas grill: It takes much less time to prepare the fire for a food that takes only a few minutes to cook. For the same reason, fish and shellfish are popular choices for stove-top grills and free-standing electric grills. Most of these open grills are smokeless, and, like an oven broiler, they give a crisp, seared exterior to fish without added oils. Because the flavor of smoke and charcoal will be missing from seafood cooked on these as well as on gas grills, the marinades and sauces used in this book are even more desirable to have in your repertoire.

## Cooking with Charcoal

### Grills

All the recipes for this book were tested using a charcoal kettle grill, although they may be cooked on any of the grills discussed in this chapter. The most important factor in charcoal grilling is learning to judge and to adjust the heat of the fire. Because so many variables affect that heat, including wind and air temperature, it's important to learn to judge how hot the fire is burning at the different stages of the cooking process. Various kinds of charcoal grills have different ways of letting you alter the heat, such as opening and closing the grill vents, raising and lowering the cooking rack, adding or removing the hood, and checking the built-in temperature gauge. Read the pertinent section below for information on your particular kind of grill.

**Kettle Grills:** This best-selling movable metal grill with its dome-shaped hood has the virtues of simplicity, affordability, and good design. It does have two drawbacks: First, the cooking rack is not adjustable, so the heat level must be manipulated by opening or closing the vents, adding or removing the hood, or moving the coals or the food. Second, it's hard to maintain a low fire for a long period of time in a kettle grill; for the long cooking of foods at low heat, the kamado works better. The kettle grill is constantly being improved, and is available in different colors and in different sizes, from one small enough to carry on a picnic to the newest deluxe version, a kettle grill embedded in a steel cart (see console grills, below). Good new features of kettle grills include enclosed ash catchers, which eliminate the mess of blowing ashes; tool hooks and a hood holder; a built-in temperature gauge; and charcoal baskets to hold coals for indirect grilling.

**Console Grills:** Larger, more expensive, and more elaborate than simple kettle grills, these rectangular grills may use either charcoal or gas tanks and may be wheeled from place to place. The cooking rack is banked by work surfaces, some with inset cutting boards, so the problem of where to put food, dishes, and utensils is solved. A variety of attachments, including an interior thermometer, a hood, and sometimes even a second rack unit, make cooking on these grills almost as convenient as cooking on a traditional range in your own kitchen.

New models of grills are blurring the line between kettle and console, and even between charcoal and gas: Some kettle grills are fueled by gas, and the newest console charcoal grill combines a kettle grill and a sturdy cart with a stainless steel work surface, a storage bin for charcoal, and an automatic gas starter. Because liquid propane gas burns cleaner than newspaper and kindling, this ignition system is an improvement over the charcoal chimney. This grill is our current favorite, as it has all the flavor and romance of charcoal, with the convenience and reliability of gas.

**Kamados:** These oval Japanese ceramic grills are more expensive and much heavier than kettle grills, but they also are more versatile. Although the cooking rack is fixed some distance from the coals, the thick walls and the shape of the kamado enable it to function as a grill-oven, much like the *tandoor* of India. It works as well as a kettle grill for the quick grilling of fish fillets and small whole fish, with the advantage that it needs a minimum of charcoal due to its insulating construction; furthermore, about 80 percent of the lump charcoal can be used a second time. The kamado has a removable interior ceramic ring that radiates heat evenly throughout the cooker, giving it the capabilities of a convection oven. Because of this double-walled construction, it retains and circulates heat from a low fire, thus allowing food to stay juicy inside. The kamado also can be used as a smoke oven by adding wood chips to the charcoal: An optional removable top piece has adjustable vents with which to regulate the amount of smoke inside the kamado, making it an excellent choice for smoking whole fish.

**Charcoal-Water Smokers:** Designed for smoking fish and meats, one of these tall, cylindrical devices is a good investment for anyone who does much sport-fishing. Charcoal-water smokers concentrate the smoke from charcoal and smoking woods in their narrow confines. They are built in layers, beginning with a fuel grate and a water pan topped by one or more cooking racks, and have adjustable vents to control the amount of smoke. Fish smoked in a charcoal-water smoker will stay moist and have the rich flavor of wood smoke. Particular favorites for smoking are small firm-fleshed whole roundfish, such as trout, and oily fish such as salmon or mackerel. Fishers will want to experiment with the catch of the day, however, and come up with their own smoked specialties to use for sandwiches, salads, hors d'oeuvres, and as a flavorful addition to casseroles and side dishes. Needless to say, smoked fish is an always-welcome food gift.

Any of the recipes in this book that use smoking woods can be adapted to a charcoal-water smoker by following the manufacturer's instructions. You don't have to have a charcoal-water smoker to add the flavor of wood smoke to your fish, however; you also can add moisture and flavor to indirectly cooked fish in any covered grill by adding water or marinade to a drip pan (see "Smoking Fish," pages 34–35).

## Fuels for the Fire

**Mesquite Charcoal:** We prefer mesquite to any other charcoal because it burns faster and cleaner than briquettes, and it also burns hotter than either briquettes or other hardwood charcoals. Mesquite is excellent for grilling fish, as it lends them its distinct though subtle fragrance. Remember to stand away from the fire when lighting mesquite, because it will send off an energetic shower of sparks; you should also make sure that your grill is not near any flammable materials. Large pieces of mesquite should be broken up with a hammer, but since mesquite catches fire and burns quickly, it's important not to make the pieces too small. Unburned lumps of mesquite can be relighted and used a second time.

Because mesquite burns at such a high temperature—up to 1,000°F—the initial stages of a hot fire may be too hot for searing or fast grilling. Generally you will need to allow at least 30 minutes for the coals to reach the hot stage (see "Know Your Fire," page 16).

Unfortunately, mesquite and other hardwood charcoals are sometimes hard to find in some parts of the country. If you love to grill, the solution is to order enough mesquite and/or other hardwood charcoal by telephone or mail to last you through the year; see Equipment and Food Sources on page 90 for the addresses and telephone numbers of hardwood charcoal suppliers.

**Hardwood Charcoal:** Other hardwoods, such as oak and ash, are made into lump charcoal. Like mesquite, they burn cleanly, with a minimum of ash, and are excellent fuels for grilling fish. They also burn hotter than briquettes, but at their hottest they burn around 800°F—not quite as hot as mesquite. Like mesquite, they add their particular subtle fragrance to food, and leftover lumps can be relighted and used again.

**Wood:** Wood takes longer to reach the grilling stage of coal-readiness (about 1 hour), and it has a higher ash content than does lump charcoal. Using half hardwood charcoal and half wood is a good way to add the fragrance of wood smoke to your food. Wood smoke will lend a strong smoky flavor to any grilled fish or shellfish. Make sure that the wood you use is whole untreated hardwood, not softwood or any kind of processed wood, including lumber, that might contain chemicals.

**Briquettes:** It's best not to use briquettes unless you absolutely have to, especially when grilling fish. Yes, briquettes *are* cheaper to buy, but because they are made with fillers and binders, they have a higher ash content than do lump charcoals, so you will need to use more briquettes for each fire. Briquettes also burn cooler than lump charcoal does, around 600°F, so they are not as effective for searing and open grilling. And, what is more important, they add chemical off-tastes to food, particularly such delicate foods as fish, and they add polluting gases to our air.

## Building the Fire

**Laying the Charcoal:** For hardwood charcoal, spread a single layer of large chunks over an area slightly larger than the area the food will cover on the cooking rack. For briquettes, spread a layer two-briquettes deep.

**Lighting the Charcoal:** If you haven't already, now is the time to give up your liquid charcoal starter. Not only does it impart its chemical taste to food—a particularly undesirable characteristic when grilling fish—but it also is damaging to the environment. And it's really not necessary—electric starters, kindling, or charcoal chimneys are just as fast, and all of these methods are safer to use, as well.

The simplest method of lighting charcoal is to use hardwood **kindling** with a wad or two of newspaper under it. Place the charcoal over the kindling, open the bottom vents of the grill, and light the newspaper (leave some air space between the briquettes and the kindling).

If you have an electric outlet near your grill, an **electric starter** may be your best choice, although it does take slightly longer to get a charcoal fire started. Place the starter under the coals and then plug it in. Remove the starter as soon as the first coals are lighted—this usually takes 10 minutes or so.

The **charcoal chimney** started out as a large coffee can with holes punched in the sides (with a beer opener) for ventilation. This device still works perfectly well, but now you can buy it in the form of a handsome tall black metal cylinder with a wooden handle. The charcoal chimney is the most popular alternative to liquid starter. Because it confines the charcoal in a smaller air space, kindling is not needed; instead, 1 or 2 sheets of crumpled newspaper are placed in the bottom section of the chimney, and medium-sized chunks of lump charcoal are piled in the top. The cooking rack is removed, the bottom grill vents are opened, and the chimney is placed on the fuel grate. Now the newspaper is lighted, and the chimney sits until the top layer of coals are lighted but not flaming. At this point, the lighted coals are dumped onto the fuel grate and unlighted coals are placed on top.

This inexpensive device will eventually pay for itself because of the money you will save by not purchasing liquid starter. It's also simpler, cleaner, and safer to use, and it's even more reliable.

Now available in natural foods stores and some supermarkets, **wax fire starters** have no additives. They are excellent for camping and picnics, when you might not want to cart along a charcoal chimney.

## Preparing the Cooking Rack

Make sure the cooking rack is clean every time you grill. This is particularly important for grilling fish; in fact, most of our recipes include instructions to clean the grill just before cooking, just to be sure that no leftover food or grease causes the fish to stick to the grill. It's important to have a wire grill brush for cleaning the cooking rack (see "Tools for Grilling Fish and Shellfish," pages 19–21). The best way to keep the cooking rack clean is to scrub it with a wire grill brush immediately *after* each grilling session—it's much easier to clean the rack when it's warm and food hasn't had too much of a chance to cook onto the metal. If you forget to clean the rack after cooking, you may need to use steel wool to get it clean once it has cooled. If so, be sure to oil it immediately after cleaning.

After the coals have been lighted, put the cooking rack in place over the coals so that the rack will be hot when food is placed on it—this will help fish cook evenly, prevent it from sticking to the grill, and give it those desirable grill marks.

Even if the cooking rack has been kept clean, you should oil it before cooking any kind of fish, and especially when cooking fish fillets or steaks directly on the rack. Having fish stick to the cooking rack is the next worst thing to overcooking it, because once this happens the flesh will tear and the fish will begin to fall apart. Most of our recipes include instructions to oil the hot cooking rack just before placing the fish on the grill. If you are using a grilling grid, a grill basket, or a fish basket, this device also should be scrubbed with a grill brush, heated over the coals, and then oiled before adding the fish to it. Use a long-handled grill brush that has been dipped in oil, or spray the rack with a vegetable-oil spray.

## Know Your Fire

Knowing the heat of the fire is especially important when grilling fish. A fire that is too hot will overcook and dry out fish, while a sluggish fire will not give fish the desirable crisp, grid-marked exterior. Most fish should be cooked over a hot fire, especially on a kettle grill, which has a cooking rack that is fixed 6 inches from the coals. Fish needs to be cooked quickly, and, ideally, it should be turned only once on the grill, to help keep it in one piece. If the fire is not hot enough, you may end up turning the fish several times to make sure it's done to your taste and also browned on the outside.

A variety of factors, including the temperature of the air and the amount of wind, can affect a fire's heat and the rate at which it burns. Learning to gauge the heat of the fire lets you know when to start grilling and when to adjust the heat for fast- or slow-burning fires and, consequently, how to adjust cooking times.

Plan on allowing 30 to 45 minutes to elapse from the time you light the charcoal until you are ready to grill; hardwood requires about 1 hour. The main thing to remember is: *Never start cooking until the flames have died down and the coals have built up a coat of white ashes.* (The one exception is that whole peppers may be charred on

the grill when the coals are still flaming.) There are three distinct stages of heat for a charcoal or wood fire:

**Hot:** At this level, glowing red coals will be covered lightly with white ashes. If you hold your hand about 6 inches from the cooking rack at this stage, you will have to move it away after 3 or 4 seconds. This is the stage for searing and for quick grilling. Be sure not to put fish on the grill if the fire is any hotter than this.

**Medium Hot:** When the fire is medium hot, you will barely be able to see an orange glow of the coals through a thicker layer of white ashes, and you will be able to keep your hand 6 inches from the cooking rack for 5 to 7 seconds. This is the best stage for covered grilling.

**Low:** At this stage, the coals are completely gray, with no visible red or orange glow. A low fire is best for long, slow cooking in a covered grill.

## Regulating the Fire

If the fire is burning too slowly or too fast for your purposes, three simple methods will allow you to regulate the heat:

**Adjusting the Vents:** Open the bottom and top vents of the grill to let more air into the grill and make the fire burn hotter. Partially close the vents to cool down the fire. (The bottom vent of a kettle grill also serves as an outlet for ashes from the bottom of the fuel grate.)

**Adjusting the Coals:** Move the coals apart to lower the heat of the fire, and move them closer together to intensify the heat.

**Knocking Off the Ashes:** If the coals have built up a thick layer of ashes and you want the fire to burn a little hotter, simply shake the grill or tap the coals with a grill utensil to remove the ashes.

If the fire is ready but you're not, put the hood on the grill and partially close the vents. This will slow the fire until you're ready to grill; then you can adjust or shake the coals to make them burn hotter.

## OPEN AND COVERED GRILLING

Most fish should be grilled on an open grill. Only when a whole fish or a chunk of a fish is more than 4 inches thick should the grill be covered. Covering the grill lowers the heat of the fire and helps ensure that the fish will be juicy, not dried out. If you are adding smoking woods or other flavor-enhancers to the coals when cooking large fish or pieces of fish, you should partially close the vents on the hood (see "Adding Flavors to the Fire," below). You also may cover the grill and partially close the upper vents if you are trying to lower the heat of the fire before adding food to the cooking rack (see "Regulating the Fire," above).

## INDIRECT GRILLING

*Indirect grilling* simply means that the food is not directly over the coals as it cooks in a covered grill. This technique makes your grill, in essence, a grill-roaster, and should be be used for large whole fish or chunks of fish that need a longer time to cook, or for smoking fish.

Our favorite method of indirect grilling uses charcoal baskets, two curved metal charcoal containers that fit against the sides of kettle grills and are included with one of the deluxe models. These baskets cannot be purchased separately, but charcoal rails that serve the same function may be. These inexpensive metal rails are designed to fit on either side of a drip pan, although they may be used without one. They keep the coals stacked up, maintaining the heat level needed to keep the coals from going out. With baskets or rails, use about half again as many coals as you would use for direct cooking. Light a charcoal chimney filled with coals and, when they are fully lighted, divide them between the baskets or rails, then place unlighted coals on top.

An alternate method is simply to push fully lighted coals to either side of the grill; in this case, use about twice as many coals as you would for direct grilling, to keep the fire from dying. We prefer to make two banks of coals rather than pushing the coals into a circle, as the coals are less likely to die out.

## ADDING FLAVORS TO THE FIRE

Most of our recipes call for fish to be cooked quickly over a direct, open fire, but smoking woods, herbs, and citrus peels can add a subtle taste to the relatively delicate flesh of fish and shellfish in only a few minutes of cooking on an uncovered grill. Smoking woods are available in bits, chips, and chunks. The most common types are hickory and mesquite, but you also will find alder, olive wood, apple, and other fruit woods. Wood bits and chips should be soaked in water to cover for about 30 minutes, then drained and sprinkled over the coals, anytime you want to add a light smoke touch to foods. Wood chunks will need to soak for about 1 hour and should be reserved for smoking fish rather than for simple grilling (see "Smoking Fish," pages 34–35).

Other flavor-enhancers for the grill are grapevine cuttings, fresh or dried herb sprigs and twigs, dried fennel branches, bay leaves and branches, and fresh or dried citrus peels. All of these, like smoking woods, should be soaked in water before being added to the fire. Use citrus peels to complement fish with a citrus marinade or sauce, and herbs to complement fish whose marinade or sauce uses the same herb or herbs. Dried fennel branches, the dried leaves and branches of bay trees (also known as laurel trees), and fresh or dried sprigs and/or branches of rosemary, sage, oregano, and thyme are among the best choices of herbal flavorings to add to your coals.

## FLARE-UPS

If you are careful not to use too hot a fire, you will avoid most flare-ups. If flare-ups do occur, move the fish to the side of the grill and wait until the fire has burned down. Partially closing the vents and covering the grill also will dampen most flames, as will moving the coals apart. Always keep a spray bottle of water handy to douse any flare-ups that don't respond to these tactics.

## COOKING TIMES

Although we have tested and timed all our recipes, our cooking times must be considered suggestions only, as so many variables affect how fast fish cooks on the grill. The temperature of the fish, the fire, and the air are important factors, as is the level of humidity and whether or not it's windy outside. On damp days, foods will cook more slowly; wind will make a fire burn hotter. As mentioned earlier, hardwood charcoal, including mesquite, burns hotter than briquettes. All of our recipes specify that fish should be at room temperature at the time it's put on the grill. This is one of the most important things you can do to ensure good grilling; it gives you more control over the length of cooking time, and will allow any food to cook more evenly. For specific guidelines on judging the doneness of fish, see "Cooking Times and Judging Doneness," page 35.

## ADDING COALS TO THE FIRE

A charcoal fire will burn for about 1 hour before it needs new coals, so most fish, including large chunks and large whole fish, will be cooked long before the fire will need replenishing. But if you are using an indirect fire that is burning much too slowly, or if your fire begins to die down, and, despite shaking the coals or moving them together, the heat of the fire does not increase, you will need to add new coals to the fire. New mesquite added to a low fire will be ready to cook over in 10 to 20 minutes; briquettes will take a little longer. Note the time that you remove the cooking rack from the fire, so that you'll know how much longer you'll need to finish the cooking.

## STORING CHARCOAL

If you do a lot of grilling, it's a good idea to buy several large bags of mesquite or other hardwood charcoal and dump them all in a large plastic or metal trash can with a tight-fitting lid. Keep the can right next to your grill, where it will stay dry and available for use any time you feel like firing up the coals.

## CLEANING THE COOKING RACK AFTER GRILLING

By far the best time to clean the cooking rack is immediately after use. A wire grill brush is indispensable for this task. Cleaning the cooking rack with a wire brush takes hardly any time when the rack is still warm. If you do have to resort to steel wool to clean a cold cooking rack, season it afterward by rubbing cooking oil on the grids.

## EXTINGUISHING THE FIRE

If you have an open grill without a cover, you should pour a little water over the coals and check them later to make sure they have gone out. If you have a covered grill, just close all the vents and cover the grill. If you have used hardwood charcoal, you will usually be able to use the leftover coals the next time you cook; to light used coals, smother them with new lighted coals from the charcoal chimney.

## COOKING WITH GAS

Although we love the flavor of charcoal and find it hard to separate it from the grilling experience, we understand why many people prefer grilling with gas. Gas grills light instantly with the touch of a button, and they heat much faster than charcoal. Gas also burns more cleanly than charcoal. Like the kamado, gas grills work better than kettle or console grills for long, slow cooking, as the temperature is automatically maintained.

Of course, when you give up the taste of charcoal smoke, you also give up the problems of lighting and storing charcoal, as well as cleaning up the ashes it leaves behind. Most gas grills also heat much faster than charcoal grills, which makes the grill process shorter and simpler, especially for foods, such as fish, that take only a few minutes of cooking. Like charcoal grills, gas grills are constantly being refined and improved. Here are some things to look for if you're planning to buy a gas grill.

## Buying a Gas Grill

Gas grills are still expensive when compared with charcoal grills, even though the more elaborate console charcoal grills are approaching some gas grills in price. And gas is cheaper to burn than charcoal: A 5-gallon tank of liquid propane gas will last for more than 24 hours of cooking and costs about $8. To find a licensed propane dealer to fill your fuel tank, look in the Yellow Pages under "Gas, Propane."

Stationary gas grills are hooked up to a natural-gas line and usually consist only of a cooking rack and a fuel box on a pedestal. Portable gas grills use refillable canisters of either liquid propane or natural gas. They range from very small grills to carry on a picnic, to large consoles with all the conveniences of a large cooking surface, shelf space, a warming rack, a built-in timer, a fuel gauge, a window in the hood, a hood-mounted thermometer, and a dual-control burner.

The burners on gas grills are individually controlled and can be set to precise cooking temperatures. They are positioned under a bed of lava rocks (a grid covered with volcanic pumice), charcoal-like briquettes, clay pyramids, metal plates, or bars; this material radiates the heat of the burner to the food. One model features porcelain-coated steel triangles that channel fat to a drip pan, which minimizes flare-ups.

The cooking rack may consist of either thin rods or wider bars; the bars act like a grill grid or basket and make it easier to cook delicate fish fillets. Most racks are porcelain-coated steel, though one model has a cast-iron rack.

Although the taste of charcoal is sacrificed for the convenience of cooking with gas, the smoke created by fat and juices dripping from the cooking food onto the lava rocks or other heat-distributing material will add its flavor to the food. Some gas grills have smokers: built-in metal compartments to hold wood chips, which add their smoky taste to the grilled foods. A smoker is not absolutely necessary, but it is a nice bonus to look for, as it simplifies the business of adding aromatic smoke to your grilling. Alternately, you can add smoking woods to any gas grill by using a disposable aluminum pie pan, or by fashioning a container from aluminum foil. Poke holes in the bottom of the pan or the container to let the smoke escape, place the soaked wood chips inside, and set the pan or container directly on the fuel bed before lighting the grill.

All gas grills have hoods, and most of them have built-in or optional rotisserie attachments to hold several whole chickens or roasts, a great convenience when cooking for a large group. Another feature to look for is a built-in side burner (like a burner on a gas stove, with its own heat control) to use for making sauces. Some gas grills have shelves that fold down for storage; others have removable shelves.

Gas grills are especially easy to keep clean. Not only do you not have to worry about handling charcoal and cleaning up its ashes, most grills can be largely self-cleaning if you use the following method: Turn the burners to high, close the hood, and leave the heat on for 15 minutes (lava rocks and briquettes should be turned upside down first). One grill has a removable bottom that can be washed in a sink.

## TOOLS FOR GRILLING FISH AND SHELLFISH

Special tools for the grill aren't absolutely necessary, but they do make grilling easier and more fun, and there are several that are especially good to have for grilling fish and shellfish.

**Charcoal chimney:** Unless you have an electric starter or an always-available stash of kindling, you should buy a charcoal chimney. You'll never have to deal with liquid starter again.

**Long-handled tongs:** These metal tongs are spring-loaded, so they have more leverage. Look for the ones found in restaurant supply stores; they are more strongly built and are reasonably priced. This all-purpose utensil is best for picking up pieces of food; it

can also be used to adjust coals, and its scalloped spoon-like tips can be used for basting.

**Wire grill brush:** A grill brush is the answer to the problem of how to keep the cooking rack clean, an essential step in good grilling that is especially important when grilling fish. A clean cooking rack prevents fish from sticking to the grill, and ensures that rancid or off flavors from other grilled foods don't affect delicate fish fillets or steaks.

**Instant-read thermometer:** The instant-read thermometer is useful when grilling large whole fish or chunks of fish that you don't want to cut into to judge doneness. Fish is done when an instant-read thermometer inserted into its center and not touching the backbone reads 140°F.

**Spray bottle:** Keep a spray bottle filled with water on hand as a last resort in putting out flare-ups in charcoal grills, but never spray water on a gas grill; instead, close the hood and turn down the heat.

**Bent-blade spatula:** The turning surface of this spatula is at a 45-degree angle to the handle, which makes this tool much easier to use and gives you more leverage when turning food. The bent-blade spatula is especially important to have for cooking fish, as it is a great help in preventing fish from falling apart when being turned. Choose the long-handled variety made for grilling.

**Skewers:** Soak wooden skewers in water for at least 30 minutes before using to keep them from burning up on the grill. Thread shrimp and other foods that tend to rotate on a skewer on two parallel wooden or metal skewers to keep the food stable.

**Timer:** Timing is critical when grilling fish. Use a kitchen timer, and reset it for each phase of the grilling process. Look for the type that clips onto your apron, so you'll be sure to hear it ring.

**Nonaluminum marinade containers:** When marinating fish, be careful never to use uncoated aluminum or cast iron. Both will interact with such acidic marinating ingredients as tomatoes, vinegar, wine, and citrus juice to give the fish a metallic off taste. We prefer shallow oval baking dishes of either glass or ceramic for whole fish, fish fillets, and steaks, and large glass or ceramic bowls for chunks and cubes.

**Grill basket:** This hinged wire basket makes it easy to turn fish, especially whole flatfish and delicate fish fillets. The grill basket should be heated on the cooking rack and then oiled before the fish is placed in it. Scrub it well with a grill brush after each use.

**Grilling grid:** Operating on the same principle as the grill basket, this perforated metal sheet sits on top of the cooking rack and is used to grill small pieces of food that would otherwise fall through the grids of the cooking rack. However, food must be turned, preferably with a bent-blade spatula, in order to grill the other side. A grilling grid is helpful for grilling whole flatfish and delicate fish fillets. A piece of metal screening is a good substitute. Like the grill basket, the grilling grid or screen should be heated and oiled before fish is placed on it.

**Cutting board:** For cutting up raw fish it's best to have a plastic or acrylic cutting board that is kept solely for use with flesh foods. These inexpensive cutting boards will not harbor bacteria as do wooden cutting boards. Be sure to wash your cutting board with hot soapy water after each use; plastic or acrylic boards may be washed in a dishwasher.

**Charcoal rails:** These inexpensive metal rails shore up stacks of charcoal on either side of the grill and are helpful when smoking fish or cooking large whole fish or chunks of fish over an indirect fire. Because the coals are stacked, they burn more steadily and are not as likely to go out as are coals placed in a circle or simply pushed to either side of the grill.

# Chapter 2
# Grilling Seafood

# GRILLING SEAFOOD

Almost any fish or shellfish can be cooked on a grill. Our twenty-five recipes include a variety of the most easily grilled and commonly available shellfish and fresh- and saltwater fish. The glossary below discusses these and other fish and shellfish, and gives suggestions for grilling. Because the best fish is the freshest fish, and because of the variations in availability in different parts of the country at different times of the year, we often list other fish that may be substituted.

Some species of saltwater fish may grow much larger than most freshwater fish, and contain more of the dark muscles that enable them to swim in the ocean. For these two reasons, most firm-fleshed, meaty fish, such as tuna and swordfish, are sea creatures. Fresh uncooked saltwater fish, unlike their freshwater cousins, have a faint briny smell of the sea, while some freshwater fish may have an earthy taste. But the real distinctions among fish are based on shape, texture, and flavor. Fresh- and saltwater fish (and those, such as salmon and steelhead, that live in both watery worlds) can be divided into two simple categories: round and flat. Small roundfish may be sold whole, cut into steaks, or filleted, while flatfish are sold whole or filleted.

Table fish are divided into categories according to texture, taste, and oil content. Their texture ranges from delicate to medium firm to firm, their flavor ranges from mild to moderate to full, and their oil content ranges from low to moderate to high. Medium-firm and firm-fleshed roundfish are the easiest to cook directly on the grill, because they are sturdier, while fish with a moderate to high oil content are less likely to dry out on the grill. But even flatfish and fish with delicate or relatively dry flesh can be grilled successfully (see "Grilling Delicate Fillets and Small Fish," page 34).

The variety of fish in the waters of our planet is huge compared with the number of domesticated animals and wild game, and the subject of fish can be a confusing one. The vagaries of availability due to seasonal variations and marketing limitations and a notoriously unfixed nomenclature add to the confusion, as does the wide variety in size among members of the same species.

The cuts of fish are simple, however: steaks, fillets, chunks, and whole fish. Some fish, especially trout, may be sold whole but boned, which makes them pricey, but easy to serve (and nice for stuffing); chunks or whole fish may be butterflied for more even grilling and easier serving. You can learn to cut up fish yourself; buying a whole fish or chunk of fish and cutting your own steaks or fillets is a good way to make sure your fish is fresh. You also can save money by learning to bone whole fish yourself, although you should keep in mind that the bone acts as a heat conductor to help the fish cook evenly, and many people think that bone-in fish stays juicier. Fish from which the skin has not been removed stays juicier because the fatty skin is a natural baster, and any skin should be left on fillets for grilling for that reason, and because the skin helps keep the flesh intact.

## FISH TERMINOLOGY

Following are some market terms for various forms of fish:

**Whole fish:** A whole fish in the fish market will have been dressed, or gutted; usually it also will have been scaled and had its gills removed. (Whole fish is sometimes referred to as fish "in the round.") You will have to remove the fins (see "Preparing Fish and Shellfish for the Grill," pages 33–34).

**Pan-dressed:** A pan-dressed fish generally is one that has had its head, tail, and fins removed for easier cooking in a skillet or baking pan.

**Halved:** A pan-dressed roundfish that has been split in half crosswise and still contains the backbone.

**Chunk:** A cross-section cut from a whole fish.

**Steak:** A crosswise slice from a whole fish.

**Fillet:** A boneless lengthwise piece of flesh cut from one side of a fish. A fillet may or may not have the skin attached, and it may sometimes contain small bones.

**Butterflied:** A pan-dressed whole roundfish or chunk that has been opened flat and had the backbone removed but the skin left intact.

**Boned:** A pan-dressed fish that has had the backbone removed but that has not been opened flat.

## A GLOSSARY OF FISH AND SHELLFISH FOR THE GRILL

### Angler

The angler achieved popularity a few years ago as a favorite of new American cuisine under the name of *monkfish.* It is also known as *goosefish,* and in Europe it is the famous *lotte,* the essential ingredient in an authentic bouillabaisse. By any name, this Atlantic species is one of the best fish for grilling, as it has firm white flesh and a sweet flavor often compared to lobster. The angler found in fish markets consists of the tail section of this large saltwater fish, and it may be cut into steaks, butterflied, or cut into fillets. Angler also may be cut into cubes for skewering. This fish is low in fat and may be paired with butter-based sauces, but it is versatile enough to be complemented by such assertive ingredients as chilies and garlic. Our recipe for angler is on page 85.

### Bass

This large family of fish includes both saltwater and freshwater varieties. All bass have white, lean mild-flavored flesh that separates into large flakes.

**Black sea bass:** An Atlantic fish with a firm, lean flesh that grills well. The black sea bass has a good flavor, similar to that of angler, and is sold whole and cut into fillets and steaks. It is interchangeable with sea bass, below.

**Redfish:** Also known as *channel bass* or *red bass,* this native of the southern Atlantic and Gulf coasts has been made famous as the Cajun dish blackened redfish.

**Sea bass:** Also known as *white sea bass,* most of this Pacific Coast fish comes from Chile. Its flesh is quite similar to that of black sea bass, and they are interchangeable in cooking.

**Striped bass:** Like steelhead and salmon, the striped bass is primarily anadromous, which means that it breeds in fresh water and lives in the sea. Some striped bass do live in freshwater lakes, however, and some are now being farmed in California. Otherwise, this fish is available only as a sport fish on the West Coast. Small striped bass may be grilled whole, like trout.

### Black cod
*See* Sablefish

### Black sea bass
*See* Bass

### Blue crab
*See* Crab

### Bluefin
*See* Tuna

### Bolina
*See* Rockfish

### Bonita/bonito
*See* Tuna

## Bluefish

A legendary East Coast sport fish, the bluefish is also available commercially, sold in fillets with the skin on. The bluefish has an oily, dark flesh with an assertive taste that is complemented by strongly flavored sauces. Because of its high oil content, it is important that bluefish be as fresh as possible. One of the best grilling fish, it is a natural with hot, spicy sauces such as our chili-mustard sauce; see page 73. Wine or citrus marinades are good treatments for bluefish.

## Brill

*See* Sole, petrale

## Buffalofish

This Southern freshwater fish has a firm white flesh and is sold cut into fillets. It may grilled like catfish.

## Cabezon

A Pacific Coast sport fish, the cabezon is sometimes available commercially either whole or in fillets. Its firm flesh is similar to that of angler and it may be substituted for that fish in recipes.

## Calamari

*See* Squid

## Catfish

The catfish is a freshwater species; what we know as *ocean catfish* is really the *wolffish* (see below). One of the most widely marketed fish, thanks to fish farming, catfish has a delicate white flesh and is usually sold in fillets. It can be grilled quickly and carefully over a hot fire; see our recipe on page 86. Although we've paired it with classic Southern dishes and Cajun spices, catfish is also good with butter-based or Asian-flavored sauces.

## Chinook salmon

*See* Salmon

## Clams

Like oysters, clams may be placed directly on the grill and eaten as soon as they open. Choose the larger clams for grilling, and serve them as hors d'oeuvres with fresh salsa or a squeeze of lemon, or serve them as part of a mixed grill such as the one on page 69.

## Cod

This saltwater fish is found in both the Atlantic and the Pacific; its family is divided into the cod, haddock, hake, and pollock groups. The flaky white flesh of the cod is delicate in taste and quite dry, so cod fillets should be cooked quickly and carefully over a hot fire, preferably in a grill basket or on a grilling grid, using a flavored butter or oil baste. Cod fillets can also be cooked in blanched leaves with a flavored butter; see the recipe for red snapper on page 74.

## Coho salmon

*See* Salmon

## Corbina

Also known as *corvina* and *drum,* this Pacific Coast fish is a member of the croaker family. Because it has a firm, moderately oily flesh with a good flavor, it holds together on the grill and is complemented by spicy sauces. It is usually sold in fillets, though you also may find small whole corbina.

## Crab

Both the small Atlantic *blue crabs* and the large Pacific *Dungeness crabs* can be grilled. Blue crabs have the advantage of being available year round, while Dungeness crabs are in season from October through May. Because their flesh is white and sweet, they are excellent with a simple sauce of drawn butter, as well as with the savory and pungent black bean sauce in our recipe for grilled Dungeness crab on page 61. Blue crabs may be substituted for Dungeness in this and most other recipes.

## Dolphin, dolphinfish

*See* Mahi-mahi

## Dorado

*See* Mahi-mahi

## Drum

*See* Corbina

## Eel

The solid white flesh of the eel is sold cut into fillets or steaks, and is found in most Japanese markets, as it is one of the prime ingredients for sushi. Because its flesh is so firm, eel is easily grilled, and its sweet mild flavor is especially good with Asian-flavored sauces such as the hoisin glaze on page 44.

## English sole

*See* sole

## Flounder

The many varieties of flounder are all distinguished by their very flat bodies and their disconcerting characteristic of having both eyes on one side of their head. Virtually all the fish sold in this country as *sole,* with the exception of the true Dover or English sole flown in from England, are really flounders. They have a white, delicate flesh and should be wrapped in leaves if they are to be cooked as fillets. Whole flounder should be generously brushed with oil or butter and cooked, preferably in a grill basket or on a grilling grid, over a hot fire for only 1 or 2 minutes per side and served immediately with a mild sauce or just as they are.

## Fluke

The *summer flounder* is also known as *fluke; see* Flounder.

## Florida pompano

*See* Pompano

## Goosefish

*See* Angler

## Grouper

Found on both coasts, the grouper has a white flesh that is mild in taste and low in fat content. Because its flesh is also firm, like that of halibut and sea bass, it may be grilled as fillets or steaks and substituted for these fish in any grilling recipe; see pages 53 and 63.

## Haddock

A smaller and slightly finer-textured member of the cod family, haddock may be grilled in the same ways as cod. *Scrod,* which are the junior version of cod, may be cooked whole in a grill basket, or wrapped in leaves as in our recipe on page 74.

## Halibut

Like swordfish and tuna, the flesh of the halibut is similar in texture to beef and maintains its shape on the grill. Because its flesh is lean, we like to pair it with butter sauces such as beurre blanc (see page 70) and flavored butters such as the one used in the recipe for grilled halibut on page 53. Grilled halibut steaks are also excellent with aïoli and other flavored mayonnaise sauces, and with romesco sauce (page 51).

## Jack

Found in both the Atlantic and the Pacific, the jack family includes the amberjack, yellow jack, jack mackerel, and yellowtail. The *jack mackerel* is very similar to mackerel and may be substituted for it on the grill. The *yellowtail* is a popular sushi fish in Japan, and because it has a moderate fat content and a firm texture, it is a good grilling fish. Look for it in the round (whole fish) or cut into fillets and steaks. Yellowtail may be substituted for tuna and ono in any recipe.

## Jack mackerel

*See* Mackerel

## Jacksmelt

A small fish usually sold pan-dressed, the jacksmelt is a good fish for grilling and may be cooked like whole trout.

## King salmon

*See* Salmon

## Lotte

*See* Angler

## Lingcod

Despite its name, the lingcod is not a true cod. Its lean, meaty flesh is distinguished by its very pale green color, but when cooked through it turns white. Lingcod fillets, steaks, and small whole fish may be grilled like rockfish.

## Lobster

The *Maine,* or *American, lobster* lives in the northern Atlantic and has meat in both its claws and its body, while the *spiny,* or *rock, lobster* (also called *Pacific lobster*) is native to warm waters and has all of its meat in its tail. They are easily distinguished, as the spiny lobster has no claws. Both kinds of lobster may be grilled; see our recipe on page 77.

## Mackerel

The strong-flavored, oily flesh of the mackerel is excellent grilled and paired with an assertive sauce; it is also a good candidate for smoking. Usually sold as whole fish up to 2 pounds in size, it is available on both coasts and should be purchased only when it is absolutely fresh, as its flavor will otherwise be too strong. The jack mackerel, which is actually a jack, is interchangeable with mackerel in cooking.

## Mako

*See* shark

## Mahi-mahi

One of the best fish for the grill, the mahi-mahi has a confusing nomenclature, also being known as *dolphin, dolphinfish,* and *dorado.* Because of the horrified reaction of tourists at seeing this fish listed as *dolphin* on menus, it is becoming more commonly known by its Hawaiian name. This large tropical fish is prized as a game fish and also is sold commercially. Because it has a moderate fat content and a firm flesh, it grills beautifully; see our recipe on page 44.

## Monkfish

*See* Angler

## Mussels

Both the *New Zealand green-lip mussel* and the *blue mussel* found on both American coasts are excellent on the grill, although the green-lip may have the advantage of being larger. Gather your own blue mussels and grill them up on a portable grill on the beach (check the newspaper or tide tables for a low tide, and make sure that no red-tide quarantine is in effect), serve them as part of a mixed grill, or cook them as the first course for a grill dinner. For cooking instructions and serving suggestions, see the recipe on page 69.

## Ocean catfish

*See* Wolffish

## Ono

Although it is related to the mackerel, the ono, also known as *wahoo,* is similar in texture and taste to tuna, which makes it an excellent fish for the grill. This large fish is found in tropical waters and comes to the mainland from Hawaii; the name *ono* is Hawaiian for "sweet." Substitute ono in any recipe calling for tuna. To grill, see page 82.

## Orange roughy

This New Zealand fish has a mild white flesh that is cut into fillets and is fairly widely available in fish markets. Related to the rockfish, it can be substituted for that fish in any recipe.

## Oysters

These wonderful bivalves are a special treat on the grill. We prefer the larger and meatier varieties, but any oyster can be grilled. The process is simplicity itself: The oysters are placed over hot coals, and, when they open, they are done. At this point you are free to gild the lily by passing any of a number of sauces, including those on page 69. If you are lucky enough to live near an oyster farm, take your friends and your portable grill with you, buy a batch of oysters, and set your grill up on the nearest beach for a special grill picnic.

## Pacific snapper

*See* Rockfish

## Pike

A large freshwater fish with lean, mild flesh, pike is usually sold in fillets that may be grilled like catfish or wrapped in leaves after being coated with butter or oil (see page 74). Serve with butter- or oil-based sauces.

## Petrale sole

*See* Sole

## Pollock

*See* Cod

## Pompano

Considered one of the best of all saltwater fish for the table, the *Florida pompano* is far superior to the *California* or *Pacific pompano.* Sold cut into fillets or whole, this small flatfish has firm, moderately oily flesh with a good flavor. Because it is thin, use an oil-based marinade or brush it with oil, and cook it quickly.

## Porgy

A small fish found on both coasts, the porgy is usually sold whole. This fish grills well and can be cooked like small whole red snapper (see page 74).

## Prawn

*See* Shrimp

## Rainbow trout

*See* Trout

# Redfish

*See* Bass

# Red snapper

*See* Snapper

# Rex sole

*See* Sole

# Rock cod

*See* Rockfish

# Rockfish

A large family of Pacific Ocean fish, often misnamed *rock cod* and *Pacific snapper,* rockfish are often sold as *red snapper* on the West Coast. The most desirable varieties for grilling are the *bolina* and the *yelloweye.* The fat content of rockfish is low, and, though their white flesh is not quite as firm as that of snapper, they are excellent grilled whole or cut into fillets; see page 51.

# Sablefish

Also known as *black cod,* the sablefish is often sold as *butterfish* on the West Coast, although it is completely different from the East Coast butterfish. Like that fish, however, it has flesh with a high oil content, making it a good choice to grill whole or in fillet or chunk form. Sablefish is also excellent smoked.

# Salmon

One of the premiere grilling fish, salmon has beautifully colored, rich meat that is high in fat content and fairly firm. The large *king salmon,* also called *chinook,* is considered the best for cooking among the various species of salmon, which include *silver* or *coho, red* or *sockeye, pink,* and *chum.* The smallest king is around 6 pounds, so you usually will find it cut into fillets, steaks, or chunks. (See our recipes on pages 40 and 47.) We are also partial to small farm-raised coho. These troutlike fish with their delicate pink flesh are delicious grilled whole (see our recipe on page 70). Salmon may be cooked until opaque throughout, or, like tuna, it may be left translucent at its center, depending on individual taste. (Northwesterners, who really know their salmon, prefer it underdone.)

# Sand dab

This small flatfish is a San Francisco specialty. It may be grilled in fillet form wrapped in leaves, or grilled whole (or pan-dressed) very quickly over a hot fire.

# Sea bass

*See* Bass

# Scallop

Although both the small *bay scallop* and the much larger *sea scallop* both may be grilled, we prefer sea scallops as they are easier to handle. If cooked correctly, sea scallops are fine grill fare. The secret is to grill them quickly over a hot fire; this ensures a lightly seared outside and a moist interior. Scallops are perfect for grilling on skewers (see page 48). A grill basket or grilling grid makes it easier to grill unskewered scallops.

# Scrod

*See* Haddock

# Shark

This fish is becoming steadily more popular as a table fish because its flesh is meaty, firm, and low in fat. It is a versatile grill fish, whether cut into steaks, fillets, or cubes for skewering. On the West Coast, shark varieties include the *thresher* and the *leopard;* on the East Coast, the *mako shark* is a highly prized table fish. Shark may be substituted in any recipe calling for swordfish; see the recipes on pages 48, 57, 58, and 69. It is not unusual for shark to have a slight odor of ammonia; this odor can be eliminated by soaking the fish in milk to cover for 30 minutes.

# Shrimp

Grilled shrimp is one of the great outdoor foods; we especially like it marinated with lots of garlic. Choose medium to large shrimp, no smaller than 16 to 20 shrimp per pound. Jumbo shrimp, which are also known as *prawns* (although the true prawn is a freshwater shellfish), can be grilled with their shells on, but we prefer the taste of slightly smaller shrimp that have been peeled and marinated. Be sure to thread shrimp crosswise on two parallel wooden skewers that have been soaked for 30 minutes in water; the shrimp should lie flat on the grill. The most important thing to remember in grilling shrimp is to not overcook them; remove them from the grill as soon as they are evenly pink and opaque, or they will be dry and tough.

## Snapper

Several varieties of snapper exist, but the *red snapper* is considered the best table fish of the group. The *Pacific snapper* is really a rockfish, while the true red snapper is distinguished by its red skin and firm flesh. This superior eating fish is usually sold whole (ranging between 2 and 20 pounds) and in fillets, and is found mainly in the warm waters of the mid-Atlantic, the Caribbean, and the Gulf of Mexico. Snapper recipes are found on pages 74 and 81. Rockfish (or Pacific snapper) may be substituted in any recipe calling for red snapper.

## Sole

Among the fish known as sole in this country are *petrale*, or *brill; rex sole; Dover sole;* and *English sole.* All of these small flatfish are really flounders, however, including the last two, which are Pacific flounders. Some true Dover sole are flown in from England, but they are relatively rare. The fish we call sole in this country are characterized by their delicate white flesh, and are marketed either cut into fillets or pan-dressed. Sole fillets should be wrapped in leaves for grilling, while pan-dressed fish may be wrapped in leaves or liberally oiled and grilled quickly over a hot fire like sand dabs.

## Squid

These inexpensive mollusks, also known by their Italian name of *calamari*, have a slightly chewy texture that can become tough if overcooked. The secret to grilling squid successfully is to marinate them in an oil-based marinade and cook them quickly over a hot fire (see our recipe on page 79). Some fish markets sell squid already cleaned, which makes grilling them even easier.

## Steelhead

*See* Trout

## Striped bass

*See* Bass

## Sturgeon

Like salmon, sturgeon is both a saltwater and freshwater fish. Its range is from Monterey, California, to southern Alaska, but the main commercial source for sturgeon is the Columbia River. Like swordfish, sturgeon has a dense, meaty flesh that grills beautifully. Sold cut into chunks, steaks, or fillets, sturgeon may be substituted in any recipe calling for swordfish.

## Swordfish

This highly prized grilling fish has a texture almost like that of steak and appeals even to those people who don't care for fish. Swordfish is sold in chunks and steaks, and is complemented by almost any kind of sauce; it's also good simply brushed with oil, grilled, and served with lemon or lime wedges. Our recipe for swordfish is on page 58.

## Tilapia

A medium-firm, mild-flavored freshwater fish sold in fillet form, tilapia may be cooked directly on the cooking rack like catfish or wrapped in leaves and grilled.

## Tilefish

Also known as *tile bass,* the tilefish gets its name from the mosaic pattern of its yellow and green skin. This East Coast fish has a low fat content and a fairly firm texture, and is sold whole or cut into fillets, chunks, and steaks. It is interchangeable with rockfish in any recipe.

## Trout

*Rainbow trout* and similar species such as the *cutthroat, brown, brook,* and *golden trout* are among the best of all fish for the grill. *Dolly Varden* and *lake trout* are really char, not trout, but they are interchangeable with trout in cooking. Due to aquaculture, fresh rainbow trout are widely available, and their sweet, moist flesh needs little adornment other than a simple flavored baste; see our recipe for grilled trout on page 43. Trout is also excellent smoked and served in salads, sandwiches, and hors d'oeuvres. The slightly larger *steelhead* trout is a prized gamefish; like salmon, it spawns in freshwater and lives in the ocean. It has a salmon-colored flesh and a richer flavor than rainbow trout.

## Tuna

Another superb fish for grilling, tuna is widely available in fillet or steak form. Its dense texture and high oil content keep it from falling apart or drying out on the grill, and its fine, distinct flavor is complemented by assertive marinades and sauces (see our recipes on pages 54 and 88). The dark red flesh of raw tuna turns almost white and opaque when cooked. Many people prefer their tuna seared on the outside and rare to just barely translucent in the center, although it remains tender when cooked until opaque throughout. Varieties of tuna include *albacore, yellowfin* (or *ahi,* the yellowfin's Hawaiian name), *bluefin,* and *bonito.* They are all interchangeable in any recipe for tuna.

## Wahoo

*See* Ono

## White sea bass

*See* Bass

## Wolffish

This Atlantic fish is often marketed as an *ocean catfish,* although its meat is more similar to that of the angler. Because its flesh is firm, it is an excellent fish for the grill, and it may be substituted for such fish as angler, tuna, and swordfish.

## Yelloweye

*See* Rockfish

## Yellowfin

*See* Tuna

## Yellowtail

*See* Jack

## BUYING, STORING, AND COOKING SEAFOOD SAFELY

Because fish and shellfish are so tender and digestible, they are also particularly vulnerable to spoiling. And because they are creatures of the water, the growth of pollution in our rivers, streams, and oceans has become a threat to seafood around the world. To make sure your fish and shellfish are as good for you as nature meant them to be, follow the guidelines below when buying, storing, and cooking seafood.

• Do not buy fish or shellfish from anyone other than a reputable fishmonger. Although fish sold by non-commercial fishers may seem like a bargain, you have no way of being sure that the fish were caught in clean waters and handled properly once they were caught. Shellfish are far more vulnerable to bacteria and viruses than are freshwater and saltwater fish; ask your fishmonger where the shellfish were gathered and ask for farmed shellfish if possible. Cooking fish and shellfish thoroughly will remove any danger of bacterial or viral infection.

• The freshest and most inexpensive fish are often found in Asian fish markets. The Chinese and Japanese are demanding and knowledgeable about fish, and you usually can be sure that fish markets catering to these consumers will have the some of best fish available.

• A large and rapid turnover of fish is one of the best indications of a good fish market, as is the cleanliness of the market and the care with which fish are handled and displayed.

• Some fish markets will cut steaks, fillets, and chunks to order from whole fish. Always ask to have this done, if possible; this will be the freshest fish you can buy.

• Whole fish should have a bright color, a clean smell, and clear, unfilmed eyes. They should be firm, not rigid or squishy to the touch. Make sure whole fish are displayed on ice and that cuts of fish are on ice or in refrigerated cases.

• Buy fish and shellfish last, bring them home from the store immediately, and place them in the refrigerator. If you know you will have to stop or that your travel time between store and home will be long, bring along a cooler with ice for transporting fish and shellfish.

• Store live shellfish loosely wrapped in paper or in a paper bag in the refrigerator until you are ready to cook it.

• Cook fish and shellfish the day you buy it. If you absolutely cannot cook it within a few hours of purchase, it can be kept for a maximum of 24 hours in a *cold* refrigerator (between 32° and 35°F).

• Remove fish from the refrigerator when you are ready to marinate it, usually right after you have lighted the coals for the grill, or about 30 minutes before cooking. This will allow the fish to come to room temperature, which will ensure that it cooks evenly.

• Do not kill live shellfish until right before you are ready to cook it.

• Never leave uncooked fish at room temperature for more than 2 hours.

• Wash your hands with soap and hot water before handling raw fish and shellfish.

• Scrub shellfish with a brush under cold running water.

• Use one cutting board, preferably an acrylic or plastic one, for fish and other flesh foods; cut all other foods on a different board. Wash the cutting board and knives in hot soapy water after use.

• Any marinade to be used as a sauce after the fish is cooked should be boiled for several minutes before being served.

• Be sure to wash in hot, soapy water any dish in which raw fish was marinated, and any vessel that was used to transfer the fish to the grill. Take care that no juices from raw fish come into contact with other foods.

• Current USDA guidelines recommend cooking all fish to an internal temperature of 160°F to be absolutely safe, but in general fish is safe to eat when the flesh is opaque throughout, or at an internal temperature of 140°F.

• Refrigerate leftover cooked fish and shellfish right away.

## PREPARING FISH FOR THE GRILL

Follow the cleanliness guidelines above. Most whole fish in fish markets have been gutted and scaled and have had their gills removed, but you may have to remove the fins. If you have caught your own fish you will need to gut and scale them, and remove the gills. If you are concerned that your fish be as fresh as possible, you may want to buy fish whole and cut them into fillets, chunks, or steaks yourself. Leaving its skin and bones intact as long as possible keeps any fish more moist and flavorful.

First, wash the fish under cold running water. **To remove the pectoral and pelvic fins:** Cut off the two fins on either side of the chest section of the fish (the pectoral fins) and the fin on the bottom of the fish, closer to the head (the pelvic fin), with a pair of scissors.

Most fish need scaling. The exceptions are catfish and eel, which must be peeled, and most trout. You can buy a special fish scaler or use a knife. **To scale a fish:** Hold the fish by the tail and scrape toward the head, making sure to remove the scales around the head itself.

**To gut roundfish:** Slit the belly from the head to the vent and pull out the entrails. Scrape along the backbone with the side of a knife to release blood pockets. Rinse under cold running water. **To gut flatfish:** Push your thumb into one of the gills or use a knife to enlarge the opening, pull out the entrails and the gill, and rinse the fish under cold running water.

Both gills must be removed from whole fish. **To remove the gills:** Open the gill cover, which is a flap of skin covering the gill, and pull out the accordion-shaped gill.

Now, **remove the dorsal and anal fins** (the dorsal fin is on top of the back, and the anal fin is on the bottom of the fish, close to the tail) by cutting on either side of the fins with a knife. Grasp the end of the dorsal fin nearest the tail and pull it toward the head; do the same with the anal fin. The bones connecting the fin to the flesh of the fish will be pulled out when the fin is removed.

Whenever possible, leave the skin on fish to be grilled. **To cut roundfish into steaks:** Use a large sharp knife or a meat cleaver and cut the steaks 1 inch thick. **To fillet roundfish:** A roundfish has two fillets, one on each side. Beginning with the tail toward you, cut down to the backbone, starting from the head and going all the way to the tail. Make a lateral cut across the fish behind the gill. Insert the blade of your knife parallel to the backbone and, making short sawing motions and holding up the top fillet with your other hand, cut down the length of the fillet. Make another lateral cut beneath the gill on the other side and, with the backbone facing up, run the knife under the backbone and cut away the bottom fillet as you did the top one. Leave the skin on the fillets for grilling.

**To fillet flatfish:** A flatfish has four fillets, two on each side of the fish. You will need to skin the flatfish, or the fillets will curl on the grill. To do so, place the fish dark-side up, make a lateral cut where the tail joins the body, and pull up a flap of skin. Holding the tail down on the board, pull on the skin to peel it off; turn the fish over and repeat to pull off the white skin on the other side. Fillet the flatfish by placing it with its eyes upward and the tail toward you. Make a cut down to the backbone from the head to the tail. Cut the upper fillet from the fish by running a sharp knife parallel to the backbone and holding the fillet up with your other hand. Cut the fillet from the fish at the tail end. Repeat to cut away the bottom fillet, then turn the fish over and repeat to cut the upper and lower fillets from the other side.

**To butterfly a roundfish:** Remove the head and tail of a whole fish, or buy a pan-dressed fish. Place the fish flesh-side down and press on the backbone; this will help to loosen the backbone. Turn the fish over and insert a knife parallel to the backbone. With short sawing motions, cut the backbone away from the fish, holding up the bone as you cut from head to tail.

## GRILLING DELICATE FILLETS AND SMALL FISH

Medium-firm fillets can be threaded on skewers or cooked on grilling grids and in grill baskets, but most delicate fillets, such as sole, should be wrapped to keep them intact and moist. The same technique may be used for any small whole or pan-dressed flatfish or roundfish. You can use aluminum foil, but charred, brilliant green leaves make a beautiful dish, and they add their own subtle flavor to fish. Use blanched large cabbage, romaine, radicchio, chard, Swiss chard, or mustard, or unsprayed grape leaves. To blanch them, plunge the leaves into boiling water for 1 to 2 minutes to make them pliable for wrapping. Remove the leaves from the pan with a slotted spoon, rinse them under cold water, and dry them with paper towels. Cut off the stems and, if the ribs are large and coarse, cut them out. Stack the leaves between sheets of paper towels until you are ready to use them.

Brush the fish with oil or melted butter, spinkle with minced fresh herbs, if you like, then wrap the fish in the cooled leaves. Close the packets with toothpicks or cotton string that has been soaked in water. Place over hot coals and cook the fish for 10 minutes for each inch of thickness (you won't have to worry about wrapped fish drying out). If you have a grill basket, just line both sides of the basket with unblanched leaves and place the fillets in the center.

## SMOKING FISH

Your covered grill easily can be converted to a charcoal-water·smoker for smoking fish. Choose fish with a moderate to full flavor, a medium-firm to firm texture, and a moderate to high oil content. Mackerel, sablefish, trout, and salmon are good fish for smoking. Start by placing several chunks of wood or 1 cup of wood chips in water to cover. Build an indirect charcoal fire in your grill using charcoal baskets or charcoal rails, or by simply pushing the lighted coals to either side of the grill. Place an aluminum pie plate or a baking pan full of water in the center of the fuel grate. If you like, you can add wine or vinegar, orange or lemon peels, or fresh or dried herbs to the water to flavor the smoke.

When the coals are medium hot, scrub the cooking rack with a grill brush to make sure it is clean, and brush or spray the hot cooking rack with oil. Dry the fish thoroughly with paper towels and lightly oil it all over. Place the fish over the drip pan. Drain the soaked wood chunks or chips well and place or sprinkle them evenly on top of the medium-hot coals. Cover the grill, partially close the vents, and smoke the fish for about 30 minutes for a whole 8-ounce fish, turning the fish once. For larger whole fish, chunks, or fillets, increase the time accordingly. Check the drip pan when you turn the fish, and add more water if necessary. Let the fish cool completely at room temperature; wrap it tightly in aluminum foil and refrigerate for storage.

## COOKING TIMES AND JUDGING DONENESS

Two visual clues will tell you when a fish is done: The flesh of the fish will begin to separate into its natural segments, and it will turn from translucence to opacity. You may, through experience, learn to tell the doneness of fish by touch; like chicken breasts, fish are done when they are firm yet springy to the touch, not soft or stiff. Shrimp are done when they turn from gray to uniformly pink and opaque; both lobster and Dungeness crab will turn red. Clams, oysters, and mussels in the shell are ready to eat when their shells open. It is much easier to tell when fillets, steaks, and butterflied fish are done; whole fish may need to be cut into. Fish is done when an instant-read thermometer inserted into its thickest part and not touching the backbone reads 140°F, but this test is necessarily limited to large whole fish or chunks.

Finally, keep in mind the famous doneness guide developed by the Canadian Department of Fisheries: Cook any fish for 10 minutes per inch of thickness (measuring the fish at its thickest point). Thus a 1-inch-thick steak should be cooked for 5 minutes on each side, and a ¾-inch-thick steak should be cooked for 3 to 4 minutes on each side. (Whole fish with the skin on may be cooked a little longer, as the skin helps to keep them moist and intact.) Although there are many variables in grilling that may slightly alter this rule, it's amazing how accurate it usually is.

## SECRETS OF THE GRILL: A LITTLE GUIDE TO GRILLING FISH AND SHELLFISH

• Observe the cleanliness guidelines on pages 32–33.

• Use a marinade or a spice paste to help season fish or, at the very least, coat the fish with oil and sprinkle with salt before grilling. Don't use uncoated aluminum or cast-iron containers to marinate fish, as the acidic content of a marinade can interact with the metal to create a metallic taste. Use glass, ceramic, enameled cast iron, coated aluminum, or stainless steel for your marinating containers.

• Remove fish from the refrigerator right after lighting the coals, or about 30 minutes before grilling, so that the fish will be at room temperature when cooked.

• Cook vegetables or any other foods to be grilled before you cook the fish. Most vegetables and many other side dishes are at their peak of flavor at room temperature, and food at that temperature is a nice contrast with fish hot off the grill. Cooking other foods first also allows you to give your full attention to the all-important task of cooking the fish perfectly.

• Make a habit of scrubbing the cooking rack with a wire grill brush before cooking fish, especially if you neglected to scrub it after your last grill session. Try to remember to scrub the cooking rack after you finish cooking each time, while the cooking rack is still warm.

• Oil the hot cooking rack just before grilling fish or

shellfish. Use a grill brush dipped in oil or spray the cooking rack with a vegetable-oil spray.

• Cover the grill and use an indirect fire to cook chunks of fish and whole fish that are more than 4 inches thick or over 3 pounds in weight.

• Reread "Know Your Fire," page 16, to make sure you know the difference between a hot and a medium-hot fire. The heat level of the fire is more important when cooking fish than with any other food. We prefer to use a hot fire when cooking on a kettle grill, which has a cooking rack fixed 6 inches from the coals. Most fish also may be cooked over a medium-hot fire, but some, such as sea scallops, salmon, tuna, and swordfish, always should be seared over a hot fire.

• *Pay attention to the cooking time!* Overcooking is the number one enemy of grilled fish. Because it's so easy to lose track of time, especially when cooking for a crowd, buy a kitchen timer that clips onto your apron. Fish goes from perfection to dry and tasteless in a matter of minutes or even seconds, so be especially watchful and don't leave the grill at all when cooking fish.

• Place delicate fillets perpendicular to the grill grids and use a bent-blade spatula to turn them, or use an oiled hot grilling grid or grill basket. You may also wrap delicate fillets or small whole or pan-dressed flatfish or roundfish in blanched leaves or in aluminum foil, or line both sides of a grill basket with unblanched leaves, placing the fish between the leaves. Medium-firm fillets may be threaded on skewers.

• Try to turn fish only once to keep it from falling apart on the grill.

• When grilling fillets with skin on one side, place them on the grill skin-side up.

• Don't stray from the grill when cooking fish. Most fish is done when the flesh begins to separate into its natural segments and the flesh is just opaque throughout. Remember: Undercooked fish can go back on the grill, but overcooked fish stays dry and overcooked.

## SPECIAL INGREDIENTS

**Asian sesame oil:** This intensely flavored oil made from toasted sesame seeds will give a smoky Far East taste to fish marinades and sauces.

**Chilies:** Medium- and full-flavored fish are enhanced by the spicy taste of fresh chilies. *Jalapeños* are small tapered chilies about 3 inches long; they may be either green or red. *Serrano chilies,* which are smaller and hotter but of a similar shape, may be substituted. *Thai chilies,* also called *"bird" peppers,* are 1½ inches to 2 inches long and very thin; they may be either green or red. *Poblano chilies* (which are called *pasillas* in some areas) are large, triangular in shape, and green-black in color. Handle fresh chilies with care: Either wear rubber gloves or make sure to wash your hands in hot soapy water right after working with chilies. Remove the seeds, the hottest part, if you're worried about the eventual heat of your sauce or marinade.

**Chili oil:** An oil in which chilies have been steeped to give it an orange color and *picante* taste. Chili oil can be the finishing touch to an Asian fish marinade or sauce.

**Fish sauce:** This salty, savory sauce is used in Thailand, Cambodia, Laos, and Vietnam in the same way as soy sauce is used in China and Japan. Although it may be an acquired taste, it can become addictive. Fish sauce is an excellent ingredient for marinades, and, combined with chopped green chilies, a little sugar, and chopped fresh cilantro, it makes an all-purpose dipping sauce that is good with any fish.

**Garlic:** We love garlic, and we especially love it with fish and shellfish. Use fresh garlic, not dried or powdered, which has an artificial taste. To simplify the peeling and chopping of garlic, use a large chef's knife to cut off the root end of each clove, then smash the cloves flat with the flat side of the knife blade; this makes the skins easy to remove. Chop the cloves by using the French technique of holding the tip of the knife down on the board with your left hand (if you are right-handed), while moving the handle up and down and from left to right with your right hand to chop the cloves evenly. Keep a paring knife at hand to scrape the chopped garlic off the chef's knife periodically.

**Ginger:** Fresh ginger is a classic ingredient in the fish cuisine of China, where it is thought to make fish taste fresher. To keep fresh ginger more than a week or so, freeze the whole piece. To use, chop off a piece about the length you think you will use, then mince it with a sharp chef's knife. (You can peel it if you like, but it's not necessary for grill recipes.) You can also grate as much of the whole root (frozen or unfrozen) as the recipe calls for. Or, you can chop fresh ginger into pieces about 1 inch thick, peel each piece, and put them all into a jar with dry sherry to cover. Keep the jar in the refrigerator, and use the flavored sherry in sauces, marinades, and stir-fries.

**Herbs:** We like to use fresh herbs when we can, especially when cooking fish. Fresh herbs are most important when you're using them in fresh sauces and for garnishes, while some dried herbs, such as thyme, sage, bay leaves, and oregano, will work perfectly well when they are reconstituted by being added to a marinade or sauce. In some cases, as for herb rubs to be spread over foods before grilling, dried herbs are preferable. There are five herbs that we prefer to use only in their fresh states, however: parsley (preferably Italian, or flat-leaf, parsley), basil, chives, cilantro, and mint. All of these seem to lose so much of their original flavor when dried that we would rather not use them at all if we can't find them fresh.

When using fresh herbs, make sure that you strip the leaves or sprigs from the stems and chop only the leaves. The stems are often woody in texture and may, like parsley and basil stems, also be bitter.

**Hoisin sauce:** Add this sweet-spicy Asian sauce to barbecue sauces and marinades. As a marinade ingredient, it will add an attractive reddish color to grilled foods. Mix hoisin sauce with rice vinegar, Asian sesame oil, and a touch of sugar to make a simple sauce for grilled fish.

**Rice wine vinegar:** A wide variety of alcohol-based Asian vinegars exists, ranging from brown rice vinegar (look for this in natural foods stores) to Chinese black vinegar. They are generally light and fresh, and may be used to balance stronger flavors and bring out the flavor of fish and other delicate foods.

**Shallots:** A great addition to many sauces and marinades, shallots are milder and sweeter than onions. Peel off the outer skin and chop them in the same manner as garlic, above.

**Soy sauce:** We use a low-salt soy sauce, available in natural foods stores.

**Tomatillos:** These green tomatolike vegetables are also called "husk tomatoes" because of their loose, papery husk. They are the basis of the Mexican *salsa verde,* and their mild, astringent taste is excellent in fresh or cooked sauces to serve with fish. Canned tomatillos are fine substitutes for fresh ones.

**Zest:** The French distinguish between the *zeste* and the *zist* of citrus fruits, and with good reason: The *zeste* is the thin, colored exterior layer, whose oils contain the intense flavor of the fruit; the *zist* is its bitter white undercoat. Whenever a recipe calls for zest, make sure that you grate only the exterior layer of the citrus fruit and don't go through to the white portion. You can also strip off the zest with a potato peeler or a zester, then mince the zest finely with a chef's knife.

CHAPTER 3

# GRILL RECIPES FOR SEAFOOD

# APPLE-SMOKED SALMON WITH ORANGE MAYONNAISE

*Grilled Apples, Beets, and Sweet Potatoes · Watercress Salad · Sauvignon Blanc*

*Serves 4*

We love salmon first of all for its rich, sweet taste, and almost as much for its deep color. This grill menu is a delightful mix of colors and flavors: The salmon is grilled over apple-wood chips, which gives it a subtle, fruity perfume, and is served topped with a pale orange mayonnaise. The apples, beets, and sweet potatoes intensify in color and taste on the grill, and combine beautifully with the salmon. Serve with a watercress salad and cold Sauvignon Blanc.

## Orange Mayonnaise

**1 navel orange**
**1 egg at room temperature**
**1 cup mild olive oil or canola oil at room temperature**
**Salt to taste**
**Orange flower water or orange essence to taste (optional)**

**1½ to 2 pounds salmon steaks or fillets**

## Marinade

**Juice of ½ orange, reserved from orange mayonnaise, above**
**1 tablespoon olive oil**
**1 tablespoon chopped fresh tarragon**
**Salt to taste**
**Freshly ground white pepper to taste**

**1 cup apple-wood chips**
**1 large sweet potato**
**2 beets**
**2 apples**
**¼ cup olive oil**
**Juice of ½ lemon**
**Tarragon or watercress sprigs for garnish**

Light a charcoal fire in an open grill. While the coals are heating, prepare the mayonnaise: With a vegetable brush, scrub the skin of the orange under running water. Grate the zest of the orange using the small shredding holes of a 6-sided grater. Cut the orange in half and juice it. Break the egg into a blender and, with the motor running, pour the oil as slowly as possible, a few drops at a time, through the open hole in the blender lid. After

pouring in about half of the oil, the mixture will have emulsified. Increase the rate of flow to a very thin stream, continuing to blend until all of the oil has been added. Blend in the zest and half of the orange juice, reserving the rest for the marinade. Transfer the mayonnaise to a bowl and add salt to taste; add orange flower water or orange essence to taste, if you like. Cover and place in the refrigerator until serving (this will help it to thicken).

Place the salmon in one layer in a shallow nonaluminum container. In a small bowl, combine all of the ingredients for the marinade and pour it over the salmon. Let marinate at room temperature until the coals are hot, about 30 minutes, turning the salmon once or twice. Place the apple-wood chips in water to cover and let them soak until it is time to grill, about 30 minutes.

Meanwhile, cut the unpeeled beets and sweet potato into ¼-inch-thick crosswise slices. Place them in separate bowls. Cut the unpeeled apples into quarters and cut a V into the center of each quarter to remove the core. Place the apples in a bowl. In a small bowl, combine the olive oil and lemon juice, and pour a third of this mixture over each bowl of vegetables and fruit. Using your hands, coat the apples, sweet potatoes, and lastly, the beets evenly with the oil and lemon juice mixture; set aside.

When the coals are hot, drain the apple-wood chips well and sprinkle them evenly over the coals. Place the apples, sweet potatoes, and beets on the cooking rack, using a grilling grid or grill basket, if you have either. Cook the fruit and vegetables for 5 to 6 minutes on each side, or until they are crisp-tender. Transfer the fruit and vegetables to a plate.

Scrub the hot cooking rack with a grill brush to make sure it is clean and brush or spray the rack with oil. Place the salmon over the hot coals and cook for 3 minutes; baste, turn, and cook for another 3 minutes, or until the outside is browned and the inside is barely translucent in the center (cook 1 or 2 minutes longer if you want the salmon opaque throughout). Transfer the salmon to each of 4 hot serving plates. Surround the salmon with the beets, sweet potatoes, and apples; top with a dollop of mayonnaise; and garnish with tarragon or watercress.

# Idaho Trout with Sage-Peppercorn Butter Baste

*Wild Rice Pancakes · Watercress Salad with Grilled Red Onion Slices · Fumé Blanc*

*Serves 4*

Whole trout is a natural for the grill, because the skin keeps the flesh moist and tender. We like it with a simple yet flavorful butter baste of minced fresh sage with ground peppercorns, with some left over to add at the table. Interesting pepper blends, some of which include allspice and juniper berries, are available in specialty foods stores, or you can make your own. Serve with wild rice pancakes and watercress salad with grilled red onion slices, and drink a Fumé Blanc. You might want to grill extra fish; boned cold trout with its slight flavor of smoke, herbs, and pepper makes a lovely salad with baby lettuce and balsamic vinegar.

**4 whole Idaho trout**

## Sage and Peppercorn Butter

**2 teaspoons mixed peppercorns (any combination of pink, black, and white)**
**½ cup (1 stick) unsalted butter**
**⅓ cup dry white wine**
**1 tablespoon minced fresh sage, or 1 teaspoon crumbled dried sage**
**Salt to taste**

**8 large fresh sage sprigs (each with several leaves), plus some for garnish**

Light a charcoal fire in an open grill. While the coals are heating, prepare the trout and flavored butter: Wash the trout inside and out under cold running water and pat them dry with paper towels. Place the trout in a shallow nonaluminum baking dish.

Place the peppercorns in a mortar or on a piece of waxed paper on a cutting board. Crush them until coarse with a pestle or a rolling pin or the side of a heavy bottle. In a small saucepan, melt the butter and add the crushed peppercorns, wine, sage, and salt. Mix well, then pour half of this mixture into a small bowl and reserve it. Brush the inside and outside of the trout with the remaining butter, and pour any butter left over from this batch over the fish in the marinade pan. Place 1 large sprig of fresh sage in the cavity of each trout, and let the trout sit at room temperature until the coals are hot, about 30 minutes.

Scrub the cooking rack with a grill brush and brush or spray it with oil, or heat and oil a clean grill basket to hold the fish. Cook the trout over hot to medium-hot coals for about 4 minutes, brushing the top with the butter in the marinade pan once during that time. Brush with the butter in the marinade pan again, turn, and cook for another 4 minutes on the second side, or until the fish are crisp and well browned, brushing them again with the butter while they are grilling.

Transfer the trout from the grill to a serving plate or plates and garnish with sage sprigs. Serve with the reserved sage and peppercorn butter to add to the trout at the table, if you like.

# GRILLED MAHI-MAHI WITH HOISIN GLAZE

*Grilled Shiitake Mushrooms · Grilled Kabocha Pumpkin or Acorn Squash Wedges*
*Spinach Salad · Steamed Rice · Asian Beer or Riesling Wine*

*Serves 4*

Mahi-mahi, or dolphinfish, has a firm flesh that grills well, and its fine flavor is complemented by the Asian ingredients in our hoisin glaze. If you can't find mahi-mahi, tuna steaks work equally well in this recipe. For a beautiful mix of colors and flavors, serve the mahi-mahi with grilled shiitake mushrooms, grilled kabocha pumpkin (or acorn squash) wedges, a spinach salad, and steamed rice. To drink, serve Asian beer or a Riesling wine.

**1½ pounds to 2 pounds 1-inch-thick mahi-mahi fillets**

## Marinade

**2 tablespoons low-salt soy sauce**
**1 tablespoon peanut oil**
**1 tablespoon hoisin sauce**
**2 tablespoons grated ginger**
**1 tablespoon rice wine vinegar**
**½ onion, minced or shredded**
**Dash Asian sesame oil**

**About 24 fresh shiitake mushrooms**
**2 small kabocha pumpkins or acorn squash**
**¼ cup peanut oil**
**2 tablespoons low-salt soy sauce**

**Cilantro sprigs for garnish (optional)**

Light a charcoal fire in an open grill. While the coals are heating, marinate the fish: Place the mahi-mahi fillets in one layer in a shallow nonaluminum container. In a small bowl, combine all the ingredients for the marinade and pour it over the fillets. Let the fillets marinate at room temperature until the coals are hot, about 30 minutes, turning them once or twice.

While the fish is marinating, prepare the vegetables: Wash and dry the mushrooms; remove and discard the stems. Cut the pumpkins or squash in half and remove the seeds. Cut the peel off the pumpkin and cut the pumpkin into 1-inch-thick wedges; cut the unpeeled squash into 1-inch-thick wedges. Place the pumpkin or squash in a steamer over boiling water, cover, and cook for about 10 minutes, or until almost tender. Place the mushrooms and pumpkin or squash in a nonaluminum bowl. Combine the peanut oil and soy sauce in a small bowl and pour it over the vegetables, using your hands to coat the vegetables evenly with the mixture.

When the coals are hot, place the vegetables on the cooking rack or use a grilling grid or a grill basket if you have one. Grill for 5 minutes on one side, then turn and grill on the second side for another 5 minutes, or until tender and well browned. Transfer the vegetables from the grill to a plate.

Scrub the cooking rack with a grill brush to make sure it is clean. Oil the hot cooking rack with a brush dipped in oil or with a vegetable-oil spray. Place the mahi-mahi fillets over the hot coals and grill them for 4 to 5 minutes on one side, then baste, turn, baste again and cook them for another 4 to 5 minutes on the second side, or until the natural segments of the flesh begin to separate and the fish is opaque throughout. Transfer the fish from the grill to a plate.

Pour the remaining marinade into a small saucepan, bring it to a boil, and cook for 2 or 3 minutes; remove from heat. Divide the fish and grilled vegetables among 4 heated plates, pour the glaze evenly over the fish, garnish with cilantro if you like, and serve.

# GRILL-ROASTED SALMON WITH VERDANT SAUCE

*Linguine with Grilled Wild Mushrooms, or Orange Risotto · Radicchio Salad with Shaved Parmesan · Sancerre or Vouvray*

*Serves 6*

The brilliant green of this sauce is a beautiful contrast to the coral-colored salmon, and this dish makes a glorious presentation for a special summer meal. The salmon is grill-roasted in a whole chunk, then filleted after cooking, if you like, for easier serving. It's also good cold, and so is a good choice to take to picnics or to serve for a buffet. At home we like to serve it with linguine with grilled wild mushrooms, and a radicchio salad with shaved Parmesan and minced garlic. It's also good with an orange risotto (made with a little orange juice and grated orange zest added to the chicken broth). Serve with a chilled Sancerre or a Vouvray.

**One 2½- to 3-pound chunk salmon**
**Olive oil for coating**

## Verdant Sauce

**1 tablespoon butter**
**1 tablespoon olive oil**
**2 to 3 garlic cloves, minced**
**2 shallots, minced**
**2 bunches spinach, stemmed**
**1 bunch basil, stemmed**
**2 tablespoons heavy (whipping) cream**
**Salt to taste**

**Basil sprigs for garnish**
**Baby yellow Roma (plum) tomatoes for garnish (optional)**

Prepare an indirect fire in a charcoal grill with a hood, using side baskets or charcoal rails, or by separating the coals into 2 piles on either side of the grill. While the coals are heating, prepare the salmon and the sauce: Place the salmon in a shallow nonaluminum container. Using your hands, coat the outside of the salmon evenly with olive oil. Place several sprigs of basil inside the salmon and let it sit while making the sauce.

To make the sauce, heat the butter and oil in a skillet or sauté pan and cook the garlic and shallots over medium-low heat until they are translucent. Add the spinach and basil, and stir until all the leaves are wilted. Stir in the cream and cook for 1 or 2 minutes longer. Place this mixture in a blender or food processor and puree until it is very smooth. Pour the sauce into a bowl, add salt to taste, cover, and set aside at room temperature.

When the coals are medium hot, scrub the hot cooking rack with a grill brush to make sure it is clean. Brush or spray the rack with oil. Place the salmon in the center of the cooking rack (with the lighted coals to either side), cover the grill, and cook for 7 to 10 minutes on each side, or until done to your liking. (The flesh will be less done toward the center; some people prefer their salmon translucent at the center, while others like it completely opaque.)

Transfer the salmon from the grill to a plate and let it cool for a few minutes. Carefully pull off the skin from both sides of the salmon. Insert the blade of a wide-blade spatula just under the top fillet and just above the bones, and lift off the top fillet, placing it upside down on a serving plate. Carefully pull the bones in one piece off the bottom fillet, and place it upside down on top of the first fillet.

Spoon enough of the sauce over the top fillet to spread it into a thin layer completely covering the fillet. Garnish the serving plate with basil sprigs, and yellow Romas, if you like. Cut the salmon into thick serving slices at the table, and pass the remaining sauce in a bowl. This dish may be served warm, cold, or at room temperature.

**Note:** The salmon chunk may also be boned and butterflied before cooking, in which case it will cook faster and more evenly. Cook the butterflied salmon flesh-side down over a direct fire in an uncovered grill for 3 minutes, then turn and cook for 3 minutes on the skin side, or until the flesh is barely translucent in the very center. Remove from the grill. Pull off the skin and place the 2 fillets on top of each other, then coat with the sauce and serve.

# SKEWERED FISH, SHELLFISH, AND PEPPERS WITH TOMATO-CILANTRO-MINT SALSA

*Yellow Rice · Romaine Lettuce Salad with Warm Goat Cheese · Flour Tortillas · Mexican Beer, Margaritas, or Fresh Limeade*

*Serves 4*

Inspired by the beaches of Mexico, this grill meal is perfect on a hot summer day. Grill each food on separate skewers to make sure each is done perfectly, then push them off the skewers and serve on a bed of yellow rice (cooked with crushed annatto seeds or saffron). Accompany with a romaine lettuce salad with warm goat cheese, hot flour tortillas (to heat tortillas on the grill, see page 66), and Mexican beer, Margaritas, or fresh limeade.

- 8 to 10 ounces sea scallops
- 8 to 10 ounces medium shrimp (16 to 20 per pound), peeled but with tails left on
- 8 to 10 ounces swordfish, tuna, or halibut fillets, cut into ¾-inch cubes

## Marinade

- 2 tablespoons oil
- ¼ cup gold tequila
- Juice of 2 limes
- ½ teaspoon ground cumin
- 1 teaspoon chili powder
- 4 garlic cloves, minced

## Tomato-Cilantro-Mint Salsa

- 3 vine-ripened tomatoes, seeded and minced, or ½ basket cherry tomatoes, minced
- 1 small white onion
- ¼ cup minced fresh mint
- 2 tablespoons minced fresh cilantro
- Juice of 1 lime
- 1 tablespoon white wine vinegar
- ¼ red serrano chili, or more to taste, seeded and minced
- Salt to taste

- 1 red bell pepper
- 1 yellow bell pepper
- Oil for coating
- Mint sprigs for garnish

Prepare a charcoal fire in an open grill. While the coals are heating, place the scallops, shrimp, and fish cubes in a large nonaluminum bowl. In a small bowl, combine all the ingredients for the marinade and pour them over the shellfish and fish. Let sit at room temperature, stirring once or twice, until the fire is ready, about 30 minutes. Place 5 long wooden skewers in water to cover.

Meanwhile, prepare the salsa: In a small bowl, combine all the ingredients for the salsa and set aside at room temperature to let the flavors blend. Cut the peppers into quarters lengthwise and remove the cores and seeds. Cut the quarters into eighths, then cut each eighth into 1-inch sections. Place the pepper pieces in a bowl and, using your hands, coat them evenly with olive oil.

When the coals are hot, scrub the hot cooking rack with a grill brush to make sure it is clean. Brush or spray the cooking rack with oil. Loosely thread all of the scallops crosswise on 1 skewer. Loosely thread the shrimp crosswise through the center on 2 parallel skewers, so that the shrimp will lie flat on the grill. Loosely thread the fish cubes on another skewer and the pepper chunks on another. Place the peppers on the grill and cook them for 5 minutes on each side, or until they are softened and charred. Transfer the peppers from the grill to a plate. Place the scallops and fish cubes on the grill. Cook them for 4 minutes on each of 2 sides, or until they are just opaque throughout. Transfer the scallops and fish from the grill to the plate holding the peppers. Place the shrimp on the grill and cook them for 3 minutes on each side, or just until they are evenly pink and opaque. Add the shrimp to the plate with the other grilled foods.

Make a bed of yellow rice on each of 4 individual plates. Push the fish, shellfish, and peppers off their skewers and divide them evenly among the plates on top of the rice. Top each serving with a little of the salsa, garnish with mint sprigs, and pass the remaining salsa at the table.

# GRILLED ROCKFISH WITH ROMESCO SAUCE AND ANCHOÏADE

*Catalonian Rice · Romaine Lettuce Salad with Orange Slices · White Burgundy or Sangría*

*Serves 4*

The firm white flesh and clean flavor of rockfish make this fish a fine choice to serve with spicy sauces. Here it is enhanced by a bright Catalonian sauce of roasted peppers, tomatoes, and toasted almonds. Anchoïade is the Provençal version of grilled bread, with the salty tang of anchovies adding its counterpoint to the grilled fish. For a Mediterranean dinner, serve with Catalonian rice (rice pilaf with chopped ham, artichokes, peas, and saffron) and a romaine lettuce salad with orange slices. A white Burgundy or sangría makes a good companion.

> 1½ to 2 pounds rockfish fillets
> 2 tablespoons olive oil
> 1 tablespoon fresh lemon juice
> Salt to taste

## Romesco Sauce

> 1 red bell pepper
> ½ cup chopped or slivered unpeeled almonds
> One 1-inch-thick slice French or country bread
>    (sandwich size)
> 3 garlic cloves
> 2 vine-ripened tomatoes, coarsely chopped
> ½ to ¾ teaspoon cayenne pepper
> Juice of 1 lemon
> Salt to taste

## Anchoïade

> 3 tablespoons olive oil
> 2 to 3 garlic cloves
> 2 teaspoons anchovy paste or mashed anchovies
> 1 teaspoon fresh lemon juice
> 1 tablespoon minced fresh Italian parsley
> Four 1-inch-thick slices French or country bread
>    (sandwich size)
>
> Italian parsley sprigs for garnish

Light a charcoal fire in an open grill. While the coals are heating, marinate the fish: Remove the fish from the refrigerator and place it in one layer in a shallow non-aluminum container. Mix together the olive oil and lemon juice and coat both sides of the fish with the mixture. Sprinkle lightly with salt and let sit at room temperature until the fire is ready, about 30 minutes.

Meanwhile, place the red pepper over the coals while they are still flaming and turn it several times to char all sides evenly; this will take about 8 minutes. Transfer the pepper to a paper bag, close the bag, and let the pepper cool. While the pepper is cooling, toast the almonds: Place the almonds in an unoiled heavy skillet over medium heat, and cook them, stirring constantly, until they begin to release their fragrance and turn golden; don't let them stay on the heat any longer, or they may burn. Remove the almonds from the heat and pour them into a bowl to stop their cooking.

Toast the bread slice on the grill until both sides are golden brown. Tear the bread into chunks and place them in a blender. Remove the pepper from the paper bag when it is cool enough to handle and carefully peel off most of the charred skin. Remove and discard the stem and seeds and place the pepper in the blender along with the toasted nuts, garlic, tomatoes, cayenne, and lemon juice. Puree just until blended; the sauce will remain grainy. Pour into a bowl and adjust the seasoning with cayenne and salt. Set aside.

When the coals are hot, prepare the anchoïade: In a small bowl, blend together the olive oil, garlic, anchovy paste or anchovies, lemon juice, and parsley. Spread this mixture thinly over one side of each slice of bread. Place the bread plain-side down over the hot coals and toast for 2 minutes or so until golden, then turn and briefly toast the other side. Place the toasts on the edges of the cooking rack to keep them warm while grilling the fish, or serve as an hors d'oeuvre.

Scrub the cooking rack with a grill brush to make sure it is clean. Oil the hot rack with a brush dipped in vegetable oil, or use a vegetable-oil spray. Place the fish fillets on the cooking rack over the hot coals and grill for 2 to 3 minutes on each side, or until the natural segments of the flesh begin to separate and the fish is opaque throughout.

Transfer the fish to a serving plate or plates pooled with a little of the romesco sauce, or pour a little of the sauce over each fillet. Pass extra sauce at the table, and serve the fish with the anchoïade, if you like.

# GRILLED HALIBUT WITH TOASTED-ALMOND BUTTER

*Grilled Asparagus · Puntette Risotto · Northwestern Semillon*

*Serves 4*

Halibut is an especially easy fish to grill, as its firm flesh stays intact on the cooking rack. Here it is complemented by a nutty whipped butter topping (whipped butter has half the calories of regular butter) and served with crisp-tender grilled asparagus. Try a risotto made from puntette (rice-shaped pasta, also called *orzo* or *riso*) for this menu: Cook ¾ cup puntette and some minced garlic in a little olive oil and butter until golden, add 1½ cups chicken broth, cover, and cook over low heat for about 20 minutes, or until all of the liquid is absorbed and the pasta is al dente. Try a dry Northwestern Semillon with this meal.

**1½ to 2 pounds halibut steaks**

## Marinade

**3 tablespoons olive oil**
**3 tablespoons lemon juice**
**Salt and freshly ground white pepper to taste**

**6 tablespoons sliced almonds**
**¼ cup unsalted whipped butter at room temperature**
**Salt to taste**
**2 pounds thin to medium-thick asparagus**
**Lemon wedges for garnish**

Light a charcoal fire in an open grill. While the coals are heating, prepare the fish: Place the halibut steaks in one layer in a shallow nonaluminum container. In a small bowl, combine all the ingredients for the marinade and pour half of it over the fish, coating it evenly; reserve the remaining marinade. Let the fish marinate at room temperature until the coals are ready, about 30 minutes.

Meanwhile, prepare the asparagus: Snap the tough bottom few inches off the asparagus spears and wash the spears. Dry the asparagus, place it in a shallow non-aluminum container, and pour the remaining marinade over the asparagus, using your hands to coat it evenly all over.

Now, toast the almonds for the almond butter: Place the almonds in a dry skillet and stir them over medium heat, watching carefully to prevent them from burning, until they are fragrant and just beginning to toast to a golden brown, about 3 to 4 minutes; remove the almonds from the heat, pour them into a bowl, and continue to stir them for a minute or so. Set the nuts aside to cool.

When the coals are hot, place the asparagus on the grill perpendicular to the grill grids and cook them for 6 to 7 minutes, turning them several times with tongs, or until they are bright green, lightly browned, and just crisp-tender. Transfer the asparagus from the grill to a plate.

Scrub the hot cooking rack with a grill brush and brush or spray it with oil. Place the halibut steaks on the grill and cook them for 4 minutes on each side, basting them before turning, or just until the natural segments of the flesh begin to separate and the fish is opaque throughout. Transfer the fish from the grill to hot serving plates.

Mince all but 2 tablespoons of the toasted almonds as finely as possible. In a small bowl, combine the minced almonds with the remaining almond butter ingredients. Top each serving of fish with a large spoonful of almond butter, and sprinkle the remaining toasted almonds on top. Accompany with the asparagus, garnish with lemon wedges, and serve.

# GRILLED TUNA STEAKS WITH MANGO SALSA

*Grilled Cornmeal Mush · Sautéed Baby Green Beans*
*Chicory Salad with Grilled Red Onion Slices and Balsamic Vinaigrette · Caribbean Beer or Fumé Blanc*

*Serves 4*

Mango salsa seems to be everywhere these days, and one of the best places for it is on top of grilled tuna. Crunchy and smooth, sweet and hot, this fresh, colorful salsa complements the rich taste and meaty texture of tuna. Serve the grilled tuna on a bed of sautéed baby green beans, with grilled cornmeal mush and a chicory salad with grilled red onion slices and a balsamic vinaigrette. (Note: The cornmeal mush will need to be made ahead and chilled for at least 1 hour before being grilled; it also may be made the day before.) Try Caribbean beer or Fumé Blanc with this meal.

## Cornmeal Mush

**3 cups water**
**½ teaspoon salt**
**1 cup cornmeal**
**Cayenne pepper to taste**

**1½ to 2 pounds ¾-inch-thick tuna steaks**

## Marinade

**¼ cup rice wine vinegar**
**1 tablespoon peanut oil**
**2 tablespoons grated fresh ginger**
**Sugar to taste**

## Mango Salsa

**1 ripe mango**
**½ cucumber, peeled, seeded, and chopped**
**¼ cup minced fresh cilantro**
**½ to 1 seeded red serrano chili, or**
   **¼ red bell pepper and cayenne pepper to taste**
**¼ cup chopped white onion**
**2 tablespoons distilled white vinegar**
**1 teaspoon sugar**
**Salt to taste**

**Cilantro sprigs for garnish**

To make the cornmeal mush: In a medium saucepan, bring the water to a slow boil and add the salt. Gradually pour in the cornmeal in a thin stream while stirring constantly with a wooden spoon. Reduce the heat to medium and cook, stirring constantly, until the mixture is thick, about 5 minutes. Add more salt as necessary and cayenne to taste. Pour the mush into an oiled loaf pan, cover, and place in the refrigerator until it is firm, 1 hour to overnight.

Light a charcoal fire in an open grill. While the coals are heating, marinate the tuna: Place the tuna steaks in one layer in a shallow nonaluminum container. In a small bowl, combine all the ingredients for the marinade and pour them over the tuna. Let marinate at room temperature until the coals are hot, about 30 minutes, turning the tuna twice.

Next, make the mango salsa: Peel the mango, then cut lengthwise slices from all sides of the fruit as close to the pit as possible; chop the fruit. In a medium nonaluminum bowl, combine the chopped mango and all of the remaining salsa ingredients, and let sit at room temperature until ready to serve.

Unmold the cornmeal mush by running a knife around the edges and inverting the pan onto a large platter. Cut the mush into ½-inch slices and brush each side with olive oil.

When the coals are hot, scrub the hot cooking rack with a grill brush and brush or spray the rack with oil. Place the tuna steaks and cornmeal mush slices over the hot coals and cook for 3 minutes. Baste and turn the tuna, and turn the cornmeal mush slices. Cook the tuna for 3 minutes on the second side, or until the natural segments of the fish barely begin to separate but the flesh is not quite opaque all the way through (or cook 1 or 2 minutes longer if you prefer tuna opaque throughout). Transfer the tuna from the grill to a plate. Cook the cornmeal mush a little longer if necessary, turning as needed, until the slices are well browned on both sides.

Place a bed of sautéed baby green beans on each of 4 individual plates, and place a tuna steak on top of each. Spoon a little mango salsa over each steak. Accompany with slices of grilled mush, garnish with cilantro sprigs, and pass the remaining salsa at the table.

# Shark Kabobs with Achiote Paste and Avocado-Orange Salsa

*Grilled Poblano Chilies Stuffed with Green Rice · Corn Tortillas · Mexican Beer*

*Serves 4*

Achiote paste has a distinctive smoky-spicy taste that adds a *picante* touch to meaty shark kabobs. Made from ground annatto seeds, achiote paste is one of the favorite seasonings in Latin American cuisine. Look for the seeds or the paste in Latino markets; either may also be found in Indian food stores. Serve these kabobs with avocado-orange salsa, hot corn tortillas, and grilled whole poblano chilies stuffed with green rice (made with pureed poblano chilies). To drink: cold Mexican beer.

**1½ pounds shark fillets**

## Marinade

**2 tablespoons annatto seeds,
 or 1 tablespoon achiote paste
4 garlic cloves, minced
¼ cup fresh orange juice
¼ cup fresh lemon juice
2 tablespoons olive oil
1 tablespoon minced fresh cilantro
Cayenne pepper to taste
Salt to taste**

## Avocado-Orange Salsa

**1 ripe avocado
Juice of 1 lemon, or more to taste
1 orange
2 to 3 garlic cloves, minced
1 tablespoon olive oil
⅓ cup chopped red onion
½ red jalapeño or serrano chili, seeded and minced
2 tablespoons chopped fresh cilantro
Salt to taste**

**Cilantro sprigs and orange slices for garnish**

Light a charcoal fire in an open grill. While the coals are heating, prepare the kabobs: Cut the shark into 1-inch cubes and place them in a nonaluminum bowl. To make the marinade, grind the annatto seeds in a spice grinder (an empty pepper grinder is fine). In a small bowl, combine the ground seeds or the achiote paste with all of the remaining marinade ingredients; mix well and pour over the shark cubes, stirring to coat them evenly. Set aside at room temperature until the coals are hot, about 30 minutes.

Meanwhile, prepare the salsa: Cut the avocado in half, remove and discard the seed, and use a large spoon to carefully scoop each intact avocado half from its shell. Cut the avocado into ¼-inch dice and place in a medium bowl. Add the lemon juice and stir carefully (the avocado should remain in dice and not become a puree).

Cut off the top and bottom of the orange down to the flesh. Place the orange upright on a cutting board and, using a large sharp knife and cutting downward, cut off the peel down to the flesh on all sides of the orange. Using a small sharp knife, cut in between the membranes to remove each segment. Cut these segments into halves crosswise. Add the orange segments and any orange juice to the avocado, but don't stir. Add the remaining salsa ingredients to the bowl and stir gently. Adjust the seasoning; it should be quite *picante*. Cover the salsa tightly with plastic wrap and set aside at room temperature.

When the coals are hot, scrub the cooking rack with a grill brush to make sure it is clean. Oil the hot cooking rack with a brush dipped in oil or with a vegetable-oil spray. *Loosely* thread the shark cubes on skewers and grill them for about 5 minutes on each of 2 sides, or until the fish is lightly browned on the outside and opaque throughout. Transfer from the grill to serving plates. Spoon some of the salsa alongside each skewer, and garnish with cilantro sprigs and orange slices. Pass the rest of the salsa at the table.

# GRILLED SWORDFISH WITH PICANTE SPICE PASTE ON BLACK BEAN SALAD

*Hot Flour Tortillas with Butter · Mexican Beer or Fresh Limeade*

*Serves 4*

The meaty texture and full flavor of swordfish is complemented by assertive tastes. In this recipe, swordfish steaks are coated with a *picante* spice paste before grilling, and are served over a black bean salad that combines the smoky flavor of grilled pepper and chili with the sweet taste of mango. Serve with hot flour tortillas with butter, and Mexican beer or fresh limeade.

**4 swordfish steaks (1½ to 2 pounds total), about ¾ inch thick**

## Picante Spice Paste

**1 tablespoon olive oil**
**½ teaspoon cayenne pepper**
**1 teaspoon ground cumin**
**Freshly ground white pepper to taste**
**Salt to taste**
**Juice of 1 lime**

## Black Bean Salad

**1 poblano chili or green bell pepper**
**1 red bell pepper**
**1 jalapeño chili, seeded and minced, or cayenne pepper to taste**
**1 small white onion, chopped**
**1 mango, peeled and chopped**
**4 cups cooked black beans (about 2 cups dried)**
**¼ cup minced fresh cilantro**
**1 tablespoon olive oil**
**1 tablespoon distilled white vinegar**
**Juice of 2 limes**
**1 teaspoon ground cumin**
**Salt to taste**
**Shredded romaine lettuce leaves**

**Cilantro sprigs for garnish**

Light a charcoal fire in a grill with a hood. While the coals are heating, marinate the fish: Place the fish steaks in one layer in a shallow nonaluminum container. In a small bowl, combine all the ingredients for the spice paste and spread half of it evenly over the steaks; turn the steaks over and spread the remaining paste evenly over the second side. Let the fish sit at room temperature until the fire is ready, about 30 minutes.

Meanwhile, when the coals are flaming and are not yet covered with ash, place the poblano or green bell pepper and the red bell pepper on the cooking rack and cook them until they are evenly charred all over, turning them as necessary; this will take about 8 minutes. Transfer the vegetables to a paper bag, close the bag, and let sit until cool to the touch, about 15 minutes. Rub and pull most of the wrinkled and charred skin off the charred vegetables. Chop the vegetables and mix them with all the remaining salad ingredients except for the lettuce. Let sit at room temperature until you are ready to serve.

When the coals are hot, scrub the hot cooking rack with a grill brush and brush or spray the rack with oil. Place the swordfish over the hot coals and cook it for 4 minutes on each side, or until the natural divisions of the flesh just begin to separate and the fish is opaque throughout. Transfer the fish from the grill to a plate. Make a shallow bed of shredded lettuce on each of 4 serving plates. Divide the bean salad evenly among the plates, placing it on top of the lettuce, then place a fish steak on top of each bed of bean salad and serve, garnished with cilantro sprigs.

# GRILL-ROASTED CRAB WITH BLACK BEAN SAUCE

*Grilled Long Beans · Bean Thread Noodles · Melon Slices with Rice Wine Vinegar and Chives · Gewürztraminer or Riesling*

*Serves 4*

Salty, pungent black bean sauce made from Chinese fermented black beans is a classic pairing with crab. We think it's even better with the sweet, smoky taste of grill-roasted crab. Serve this gloriously messy dish over plates of bean thread noodles, along with grilled long beans, and melon slices (cantaloupe, crenshaw, and honeydew) sprinkled with rice wine vinegar and minced fresh chives. Serve a Gewürztraminer or a Riesling, and make sure you have fingerbowls and lots of napkins.

**2 large live Dungeness crabs**

## Black Bean Sauce

**¼ cup black bean–garlic sauce (available in Asian markets)**
**2 tablespoons peanut oil**
**¼ cup rice wine vinegar**
**¼ cup chopped fresh cilantro**
**½ teaspoon chili oil, or to taste (optional)**

**1 pound Chinese long beans or green beans**
**Peanut oil for coating**
**Cilantro sprigs for garnish**

Keep the crabs loosely wrapped in paper in the refrigerator until you are ready to cook them. Light a charcoal fire in a grill with a hood. While the coals are heating, prepare the sauce: In a small bowl, combine all of the ingredients for the sauce; set aside. Place the beans in a large, shallow container and drizzle a little peanut oil over them. Using your hands, coat the beans evenly with the oil; set aside.

When the coals are hot, kill the crabs by hitting them hard between the eyes against the sharp edge of a kitchen counter. Rinse them under cold running water, place them upside down on a cutting board, and cut them in half down the middle using a large Chinese cleaver or by hitting the back of a large French chef's knife with a hammer. Pull off and discard the spongy gray gills and remove the crooked white intestine found along the center of the back. Scoop out the yellow crab butter and add it to the black bean sauce. Rinse the crab again, and cut off each leg together with the adjoining body section. Using a hammer, lightly crack the shells of the legs evenly all over.

Place the crab pieces in a large nonaluminum bowl and pour half of the black bean sauce over them, reserving the other half. Using your hands, coat the pieces evenly with the sauce.

Place the beans perpendicular to the grill grids over the hot fire and cook for for 8 to 10 minutes, turning frequently, or until they are slightly wrinkled and browned. Transfer the beans from the grill to a large serving platter.

Place the crab pieces on the grill, cover the grill, and cook the crab for 3 to 4 minutes. Turn the crab pieces, baste with the sauce in the marinade bowl, cover the grill again, and cook the crab 3 to 4 minutes longer, or until the shells are bright red and the flesh is opaque.

Transfer the crab to the serving platter with the beans, garnish with cilantro, and serve with plates of hot bean thread noodles. Pass the reserved black bean sauce at the table to dip the crab meat in.

# THAI BARBECUED SEA BASS ON A BED OF GREEN PAPAYA SALAD

*Grilled Japanese Eggplant · Sticky Rice · Thai Beer*

*Serves 4*

Both Atlantic black sea bass and Pacific white, or Chilean, sea bass have a white, sweet flesh that is complemented by this flavorful Thai-inspired marinade and dipping sauce. Serve the fish over a bed of tart-sweet green papaya salad (use a mixture of green and red cabbage if you can't find green papaya), accompanied with sticky rice and grilled Japanese eggplant. Thai beer is perfect with this meal.

## Marinade

    **2 tablespoons peanut oil**
    **1 teaspoon low-salt soy sauce**
    **4 green onions, minced**
    **2 to 4 tablespoons fish sauce**
    **2 tablespoons chopped fresh cilantro**
    **8 Thai chilies, slit through with stem intact, or**
        **1 jalapeño chili with seeds, minced**

    **1½ to 2 pounds sea bass fillets**
    **4 large Japanese eggplants**
    **Peanut oil for coating**

## Green Papaya Salad

    **1 unpeeled green papaya, shredded**
    **1 carrot, peeled and shredded**
    **1 jalapeño chili, seeded and minced**
    **½ small red onion, cut into thin slivers**
    **1 tablespoon sugar or to taste**
    **1 tablespoon fish sauce**
    **2 tablespoons rice wine vinegar**
    **1 tablespoon fresh lime juice**
    **¼ cup minced fresh cilantro**
    **¼ cup roasted peanuts, chopped**

    **Cilantro sprigs for garnish**

Light a charcoal fire in an open grill. While the coals are heating, marinate the fish: In a small bowl, combine all the ingredients for the marinade. Place the fish fillets in one layer in a shallow nonaluminum container. Pour half of the marinade over the fish, reserving the remaining half to use as a table sauce. Let sit at room temperature until the fire is ready, about 30 minutes, turning the fish 2 or 3 times.

Meanwhile, prepare the Japanese eggplant: Cut each one into ¼-inch lengthwise slices up to but not through the top of the eggplant; fan out the slices as much as possible. Using your hands, rub the cut surfaces and the skin of the eggplant evenly all over with peanut oil; set aside.

Next, make the green papaya salad: In a medium bowl, combine all the ingredients for the salad and set aside at room temperature.

When the coals are hot, grill the eggplant for 5 to 7 minutes on each side, or until it is well browned and tender. Transfer the eggplant from the grill to a plate.

Scrub the hot cooking rack with a grill brush and brush or spray the rack with oil. Grill the sea bass over the hot coals for 4 minutes on each side, basting with the marinade before turning. The fish should be golden brown on both sides, opaque throughout, and just beginning to separate into its natural divisions. Transfer the fish from the grill to a plate.

Place a fanned-out eggplant on each of 4 individual plates, and divide the green papaya salad evenly among the plates. Place 1 serving of fish on each bed of salad, top with a spoonful of the reserved marinade, and garnish with cilantro sprigs. Pass the remaining reserved marinade at the table.

# GARLIC SHRIMP WITH GRILLED OKRA AND FETA-STUFFED TOMATOES

*Black-eyed Peas with Minced Red Bell Pepper* · *Microbrewed Beer or Chardonnay*

*Serves 4*

Something special happens to shrimp on the grill, and skewered garlic shrimp is one of our all-time favorite foods, especially on a hot summer day. Serve these crisp-tender shellfish over a bed of black-eyed peas with minced red bell pepper, accompanied with grilled okra and grilled tomatoes with feta cheese. (Okra is surprisingly good grilled—in fact, we promise that even people who don't like okra will like it cooked this way.) Microbrewed beer or a fine Chardonnay make good companions. (Garlic shrimp are also good over a bed of black bean salad; see page 58).

**1½ pounds medium shrimp (about 16 to 18 to a pound)**

## Marinade

**3 tablespoons olive oil**
**Juice of 2 limes**
**1 jalapeño chili, seeded and minced**
**6 garlic cloves, minced**

**4 ripe tomatoes**
**2 ounces feta cheese, crumbled, about ½ cup**
**1 tablespoon chopped fresh thyme**
**Olive oil**
**About 20 large okra**
**Thyme sprigs for garnish**

Light a charcoal fire in a grill with a hood. While the coals are heating, prepare the shrimp: Place 8 wooden skewers in water to cover. Peel the shrimp, leaving the tails attached. Place the shrimp in a nonaluminum bowl. Combine all of the marinade ingredients in a small bowl and pour them over the shrimp. Marinate at room temperature until the fire is ready, about 30 minutes.

Meanwhile, prepare the vegetables: Cut the tomatoes in half and, cupping the halves one at a time in the hollow of your hand, shake and slightly squeeze the tomatoes upside down over a sink to remove the seeds. With a spoon, remove the pulp from the center of each tomato. Place the feta cheese in a small bowl and mix in the chopped thyme. Dividing the feta cheese evenly among the tomatoes, spoon it into the centers. Drizzle a little olive oil over the top of the cheese.

Pour a little olive oil on your hands and use it to coat the outside of the tomatoes evenly; set the tomatoes aside. Place the okra on a plate and, using your hands again, coat them evenly all over with olive oil.

When the coals are hot, place the tomato halves and okra to the side of the cooking rack and cook for 4 minutes, then cover the grill and cook them for another 2 to 4 minutes, or until the okra is brown and crisp and the tomatoes are beginning to wrinkle on the outside. Transfer the vegetables from the grill to a plate.

Loosely thread 4 equal batches of shrimp crosswise through the center on double skewers (this keeps them from turning on the grill). Place the skewers over the hot coals and cook for 3 minutes on each side, or just until the shrimp are evenly pink and opaque. Transfer the skewers to a plate. Serve 1 double skewer per serving on a bed of black-eyed peas, accompanied with the tomatoes and okra, and garnished with thyme sprigs.

# FISH TACOS WITH ROASTED-PEPPER SAUCE AND SALSA VERDE

*Black Beans · Shredded Romaine Lettuce · Black Rice · Corn Tortillas · Avocado and Mango Salad · Mexican Beer*

*Serves 4*

In this recipe, snapper is given a quick, light marinade and grilled up for tacos to be topped with a salsa of grilled tomatillos and a smooth red pepper sauce. Accompany with black beans and shredded romaine lettuce to add to the tacos, and serve with cold Mexican beer, black rice (made with the black bean broth), and a salad of ripe avocado and mango slices.

## Marinade

2 tablespoons minced fresh cilantro
¼ cup corn oil
Juice of 1 lime
1 teaspoon ground cumin
½ small red onion, minced

1 pound snapper fillets
1 red bell pepper
1½ cups fresh tomatillos (optional)
8 corn tortillas, preferably handmade

## Salsa Verde

Grilled fresh tomatillos (above), or 1½ cups
   drained canned tomatillos
¾ cup cherry tomatoes, coarsely chopped (optional)
¼ cup minced fresh cilantro
Juice of 1 to 2 limes
1 tablespoon olive oil
¼ cup chopped white onion
Salt to taste

## Roasted-Pepper Sauce

1 roasted red bell pepper (above)
1 tablespoon mayonnaise, plain yogurt, or sour cream
1 tablespoon olive oil
Salt to taste

Shredded romaine lettuce leaves
Cooked black beans
Cilantro sprigs for garnish

Light a charcoal fire in a grill with a hood. While the coals are heating, prepare the fish: Combine all the ingredients for the marinade in a small bowl. Place the snapper fillets in a shallow nonaluminum container, pour the marinade over them, and let sit at room temperature until the coals are hot, turning the fish once or twice.

When the coals are flaming but not yet covered with ash, roast the red pepper and the fresh tomatillos (if using) for the two sauces: Place the red pepper in the center of the cooking rack over the coals, and place the fresh tomatillos on the edges of the cooking rack. Cook, turning as necessary, until the tomatillos are lightly charred and tender and the bell pepper is evenly charred all over, about 8 minutes. Transfer the tomatillos to a plate and set them aside; transfer the pepper to a paper bag, close it, and let it sit until cool enough to handle.

While the vegetables are cooling, lightly sprinkle with water the top and bottom tortillas in the stack of tortillas, wrap the tortillas in aluminum foil, and place them to the side of the cooking rack; cover the grill and let the tortillas heat while the sauces are being made.

To make the salsa: When the tomatillos are cool enough to touch, pull off their papery husks, leaving any charred flesh, and chop the tomatillos coarsely on a cutting board. If you are using canned tomatillos, chop them coarsely. Place the tomatillos in a bowl, add the remaining salsa ingredients, and set aside at room temperature.

To make the roasted-pepper sauce: Pull most of the charred skin off the pepper, leaving some charred bits, then cut the pepper in half and remove the stem and seeds. Place the pepper in a blender. Add the mayonnaise, yogurt, or sour cream and oil to the blender and blend at high speed, scraping down the sides as necessary, until the pepper is pureed as smoothly as possible. Pour the sauce into a bowl, add salt, and set aside.

Scrub the center of the hot cooking rack with a grill brush and brush or spray the rack with oil. Turn the tortilla packet, then grill the snapper for 3 to 4 minutes on one side; turn the snapper, and grill for 3 to 4 minutes on the second side, or until the natural divisions of the flesh begin to separate and the fish is opaque throughout.

Transfer the snapper to a cutting board and chop it coarsely. Serve the chopped fish on a platter with a mound of shredded lettuce, a bowl of beans, and a mound of cilantro sprigs. Accompany with the hot tortillas, the pepper sauce, and the salsa, and let each guest construct his or her own tacos.

# MIXED SEAFOOD GRILL

*Sauce Verte · Homemade Chili Sauce · Rice Salad on a Bed of Watercress · French Bread · Chardonnay*

*Serves 4*

A mixed seafood grill can consist of any of your favorite fish and shellfish, and can serve as a first course or as a main dish. Other good choices besides the seafood listed below are clams, scallops, and salmon or tuna steaks. Sauce verte and our homemade chili sauce are fast and simple to make. You may want to add a third sauce, or choose two or three sauces from elsewhere in this book. For main-course accompaniments, we like a rice salad made with parsley, pine nuts, and olives served on a bed of watercress, and lots of crusty French bread. To drink: the best Chardonnay you can afford.

**8 large oysters in the shell**
**8 large New Zealand green-lip mussels or blue mussels**
**8 jumbo shrimp**
**2 spiny (rock) lobsters or defrosted frozen lobster tails**
**1 pound mako shark or other firm-fleshed white fish fillets**
**Olive oil for coating**

## Sauce Verte

**3 garlic cloves, minced**
**2 tablespoons minced fresh Italian parsley**
**1 tablespoon minced fresh tarragon or chervil**
**1 tablespoon drained capers**
**1 tablespoon white wine vinegar**
**6 tablespoons olive oil**
**Salt and freshly ground white pepper to taste**

## Homemade Chili Sauce

**4 vine-ripened Roma (plum) tomatoes, or**
**  1 basket cherry tomatoes, chopped**
**1 white onion, chopped**
**½ jalapeño chili, stemmed, seeded, and minced**
**¼ cup water**
**1 teaspoon chili powder, or to taste**
**2 tablespoons distilled white vinegar, or more to taste**
**½ teaspoon sugar**
**1 garlic clove, minced**
**Salt to taste**
**Lemon wedges and parsley sprigs for garnish**

Light a charcoal fire in an open grill. While the coals are heating, soak 4 long wooden skewers in water to cover until time to grill. Next, prepare the fish and shellfish: Scrub the oysters and mussels under cold running water and pull the stringy black beards off the mussels. Rinse the shrimp and lobsters under cold water. Peel and devein the shrimp. Cut the heads away from the lobsters and split the tails in half lengthwise. Cut the mako or other fish into 1-inch cubes. Coat the shrimp, lobsters, and fish with olive oil and set them aside with the oysters and mussels until the coals are hot, about 30 minutes.

Meanwhile, make the sauces. To make the sauce verte: Combine all the ingredients in a small bowl and adjust the seasoning; set aside at room temperature.

To make the chili sauce: Place the tomatoes, onion, jalapeño, and water in a small nonaluminum saucepan. Cook over medium-low heat for about 10 minutes, or until the tomatoes break down to make a thick sauce. Add the remaining ingredients and cook for another 5 minutes, stirring occasionally. Adjust the seasoning and set the sauce aside at room temperature.

When the coals are hot, scrub the hot cooking rack with a grill brush and brush or spray it with oil. Loosely thread 4 shrimp through the center on 2 pairs of parallel skewers so the shrimp will lie flat on the grill. Loosely thread the fish cubes on 2 separate skewers.

Place the fish kabobs over the hot coals and cook them for about 5 minutes on each of 2 sides, or until opaque throughout; transfer them from the grill to a plate. Place the shrimp on the grill and cook them for 3 minutes on each side, or until evenly pink and opaque; transfer them from the grill to a plate. Place the lobster tails on the grill and cook them flesh-side down for 3 to 4 minutes, then turn and cook them for 2 to 3 minutes, or until the shells are red and the flesh is opaque. Transfer the lobster from the grill to a plate. Place the oysters and mussels on the grill and cook them for several minutes until all the shells open; carefully transfer them to a plate. Push the shrimp and fish cubes off the skewers and serve each guest a mix of fish and shellfish, with the sauces alongside in individual bowls. Garnish with lemon wedges and parsley sprigs.

# GRILLED COHO SALMON WITH BASIL BEURRE BLANC

*Grilled Zucchini · Angel Hair Pasta with Garlic and Olive Oil · Soave or Frascati*

*Serves 4*

Coho salmon is one of our favorite fish; the flesh is moderately firm and sweet like that of trout, but with the color of salmon. Because they are farmed, small coho are becoming more available. Here we match coho with a basil beurre blanc for the contrast in colors and the complementary flavors. Because the classic beurre blanc is luxurious both in taste and in calories, we've lightened our version with yogurt. Serve this dish with grilled whole baby zucchini (or medium zucchini that have been sliced lengthwise with the stem end still attached and then fanned open) and angel hair pasta with a simple sauce of a little minced garlic cooked in olive oil and reduced chicken broth. To drink, try a chilled Soave or a Frascati.

**4 pan-dressed coho salmon, about 12 ounces each**
**Olive oil for coating**
**Salt to taste**

## Basil Beurre Blanc

**¼ cup dry white wine**
**2 shallots, minced**
**4 tablespoons chilled butter, cut into small pieces**
**¼ cup packed fresh basil leaves**
**¼ cup plain yogurt**
**Salt to taste**

**Basil leaves for garnish**

Light a charcoal fire in an open grill. While the coals are heating, place the fish in a shallow nonaluminum container and coat them all over with olive oil. Let the fish sit at room temperature until the coals are hot, about 30 minutes.

About 15 minutes before grilling the fish, make the beurre blanc: Place the wine and shallots in a small nonaluminum pan. Cook and stir the mixture over medium-low heat until the liquid has almost completely evaporated; watch carefully to make sure it does not scorch. Remove the mixture from heat and let it cool for about 3 minutes. Meanwhile, place the basil and yogurt in a blender and puree until very smooth. Transfer the puree from the blender to a small bowl.

Using a small whisk, beat the butter 1 or 2 pieces at a time into the reduced wine and shallot mixture to make a thick sauce. Whisk in the basil and yogurt puree. Set aside in larger pan of barely hot water to keep very slightly warm.

When the coals are hot, scrub the hot cooking rack with a grill brush and brush or spray it with oil. Place the coho on the grill and cook them for 3 to 4 minutes on each side, or until the flesh is opaque throughout. Transfer from the grill to a plate. Dividing the sauce evenly among 4 heated plates, make a pool of basil beurre blanc on each plate. Place 1 fish on top of each pool of sauce, garnish with basil leaves, and serve at once.

# GRILLED BLUEFISH WITH CHILI-MUSTARD SAUCE

*Grilled Radicchio · Grilled Polenta · Green Salad with Baby Roma Tomatoes · Grilled Jalapeños · Beer*

*Serves 4*

Bluefish has an oily, strongly flavored flesh that is excellent grilled and is complemented by assertive sauces such as our mustard sauce with grilled jalapeño. Hardy souls may want to grill extra chilies and serve them as appetizers (with grilled bread or polenta) or to garnish the fish. Good accompaniments for grilled bluefish are grilled radicchio wedges (brush them with oil first), grilled polenta slices, and a green salad with baby Roma tomatoes. To drink: your favorite beer.

**1½ to 2 pounds bluefish fillets**

## Chili-Mustard Sauce

**1 jalapeño chili**
**2 tablespoons whole-grain mustard**
**2 tablespoons Dijon mustard**
**3 tablespoons olive oil**
**1½ tablespoons white wine vinegar**
**Salt to taste**

## Grilled Jalapeños (optional)

**8 jalapeño chilies**
**2 tablespoons olive oil mixed with 2 tablespoons distilled white vinegar**

Light a charcoal fire in an open grill. While the coals are heating, prepare the fish: Place the bluefish fillets in one layer in a shallow nonaluminum container and set them aside at room temperature while you prepare the sauce.

While the coals are still flaming, place the jalapeño on the cooking rack. If you want extra jalapeños for garnish or appetizers, put them on the grill too. Cook, turning several times, until lightly browned on all sides. Stem, seed, and mince the jalapeño to be used in the sauce, and place the optional grilled jalapeños in a bowl and toss them with the oil and vinegar. (Please note: These are *hot*.)

To make the sauce, combine the minced jalapeño and all the remaining ingredients in a small bowl. Using about half of the sauce, coat the fish evenly with the sauce on both sides; reserve the remaining sauce. Let the fish sit at room temperature until the coals are hot, about 30 minutes.

When the coals are hot, scrub the hot cooking rack with a grill brush and brush or spray the rack with oil. Place the bluefish fillets over the hot coals and grill them for about 5 minutes on each side, or until the flesh is opaque throughout. Transfer the fish from the grill to heated serving plates. Garnish with the optional jalapeños, if you like, and top each serving with a little of the reserved sauce, or pass the sauce alongside.

# WHOLE RED SNAPPERS GRILLED IN LEAVES WITH GARLIC-HERB BUTTER

*Lemon Risotto · Grilled Fennel · Country Bread · Muscadet*

*Serves 4*

Grilling fish in leaves not only makes an especially beautiful dish, it also keeps fish moist and tender, and adds a subtle taste of leafy greens to the flavors of fish and charcoal. Although we've used it here with the fairly firm-textured red snapper, this technique is one of the best ways to grill tender-fleshed fillets and any small whole or pan-dressed roundfish or flatfish. In this recipe, an intense compound butter adds extra flavor to the fish. Serve this dish with a lemon risotto (use both fresh juice and grated zest), grilled fennel, and a country bread.. To drink: a chilled Muscadet.

**Four 1-pound pan-dressed red snappers**
**About 4 to 12 chard, Swiss chard, mustard, cabbage, radicchio, romaine lettuce, or grape leaves, depending on size (try to find the largest leaves possible)**

## Garlic-Herb Butter

**5 garlic cloves, minced**
**3 tablespoons minced fresh parsley**
**2 tablespoons minced fresh oregano**
**2 teaspoons fresh lemon juice**
**4 tablespoons unsalted butter at room temperature**
**Salt and freshly ground white pepper to taste**

**Oregano sprigs for fish, fire, and garnish**
**Lemon wedges for garnish**

Light a charcoal fire in an open grill. While the coals are heating, prepare the fish: Rinse the snappers under cold running water, then dry them as thoroughly as possible inside and out with paper towels. Set aside.

Stem the leaves. If the ribs of the leaves are large and coarse, cut them out and discard. In a large pot of boiling water, blanch the leaves for 1 to 2 minutes; carefully remove them from the pot with a slotted spoon and rinse them under cold water. Thoroughly dry the leaves and stack them flat between layers of paper towels.

Next, make the butter: In a mortar, grind the garlic and herbs into a paste with a pestle. Stir in the lemon juice and blend in the butter. Add the salt and pepper. Dividing this butter evenly among the fish, spread it over both sides and on the inside of each fish. Place an oregano sprig inside each fish. Wrap the leaves around the fish, overlapping them as necessary to cover the fish completely and folding in the sides to keep the butter from leaking out. Fasten the leaves closed with toothpicks. Soak a small handful of oregano sprigs and any leftover stems in water.

When the coals are hot, drain the oregano sprigs and sprinkle them evenly over the coals. Place the fish on the grill and cook them for 3 to 4 minutes on each side, or until the leaves are bright green and partly charred. Transfer the fish from the grill and serve them wrapped in their leaves and garnished with oregano and lemon wedges.

# GRILLED LOBSTER WITH LEMON-THYME BUTTER

*Grilled Baby Red Potatoes · Grilled Baby Artichokes · Foccacia with Green Onions, or Sweet French Bread · Chardonnay*

*Serves 4*

What could be better than sweet, faintly smoky lobster meat dipped in fragrant melted butter? Lemon-thyme butter is equally good drizzled over grilled baby red potatoes and baby artichokes. Either Maine lobsters or spiny (rock) lobsters can be grilled. We like focaccia with green onions, or sweet French bread, to clean our plates with, and a good oaky Chardonnay to drink.

> **Four 2- to 2½-pound live lobsters**
> **About 20 baby artichokes, halved**
> **About 20 baby red potatoes, halved if more than**
>    **1 inch in diameter**
> **Olive oil for coating**

## Lemon–Thyme Butter

> **½ cup (1 stick) unsalted butter, melted**
> **2 to 3 garlic cloves, minced**
> **2 tablespoons chopped fresh thyme**
> **Juice of ½ lemon**
> **Salt to taste**
> **Roe and/or tomalley from lobster (optional)**
>
> **Thyme sprigs and lemon wedges for garnish**

Keep the live lobsters loosely wrapped in paper in the refrigerator until you are ready to grill them. Light a charcoal fire in a grill with a hood. While the coals are heating, parboil the artichokes and potatoes in boiling water for 5 minutes. Drain and dry them well on paper towels. Place the artichokes and potatoes in a shallow container and coat them evenly with olive oil, using your hands. Make the lemon-thyme butter by combining all the ingredients in a small bowl.

When the coals are hot, place the vegetables on a grilling grid or in a grill basket, or thread them on metal skewers. Place the vegetables on the cooking rack, cover the grill, and cook them for 5 minutes on each side, or until browned and tender. Transfer the vegetables to a serving plate and set them aside.

Immediately before grilling them, kill the lobsters by plunging a knife between their eyes or into the back of the shell where the chest and tail meet. Quickly rinse and dry the lobsters (they may keep moving), and cut them completely in half using a large cleaver or a French chef's knife. Remove and discard the gray intestinal tract, the gills, and the sand sac. Remove any coral (roe) and/or green tomalley (liver), and add them to the lemon-thyme butter, if you like. Brush the lobsters all over with the lemon-thyme butter.

Place the lobsters split-side down over the hot coals and sear them for 3 to 4 minutes; baste, turn, and cook them for 3 to 4 minutes on the second side. Baste and turn the lobsters split-side down again, cover the grill, and cook for 2 to 3 minutes, or until the shells are bright red and the flesh is opaque.

Transfer the lobsters to a serving plate and surround them with the grilled potatoes and artichokes. Garnish the plate with sprigs of thyme and wedges of lemon, and pass the remaining lemon-thyme butter to dip the lobster in and to drizzle over the vegetables.

# GRILLED SQUID AND SCALLOPS OVER BLACK FETTUCCINE

*Oakleaf Lettuce Salad · Italian Country Bread · Bordeaux*

*Serves 4*

This strikingly beautiful dish is easy to make: All of the toppings for the pasta are quickly grilled, then briefly heated with garlic and oil, and poured over the hot pasta. The taste of charcoal and the slight charring of the shellfish and vegetables make this a special dish to serve with an oakleaf lettuce salad, Italian country bread, and a light red wine such as a Bordeaux. If you can't find black fettuccine, which gets its color from the ink of the squid, look for saffron, tomato, or spinach fettuccine.

**12 ounces squid**
**Olive oil for coating, plus 3 tablespoons**
**12 ounces sea scallops**
**8 ounces sugar snap peas**
**2 red bell peppers**
**1 tablespoon salt**
**1 pound dried black fettuccine**
**4 garlic cloves**
**¼ cup chicken broth**
**¼ teaspoon dried red pepper flakes, or to taste**
**2 tablespoons minced fresh basil**

Prepare a charcoal fire in an open grill. While the coals are heating, prepare the squid: Buy squid that have already been cleaned, or clean them yourself as follows: Cut off the tentacles just above the head of each squid; cut off the head and discard it. Squeeze out the hard round bone at the end of the tentacles. Press along the length of the body and squeeze out the entrails, then pull out the long narrow bone that protrudes from the body. Rinse the bodies (inside and out) and tentacles. Dry the squid pieces thoroughly on paper towels. Using your hands, coat them evenly with olive oil and set them aside.

Dry the scallops with paper towels and coat them with olive oil using your hands. Trim the peas and coat them with oil in the same way. Cut the peppers into fourths, remove the stems and seeds, and coat the peppers with olive oil also.

When the coals are hot, set a large pot of water to boil on the stove and add the salt. Place the squid, scallops, peas, and peppers on a grilling grid, a piece of metal screening, or in a grill basket. Grill them over the hot coals for 4 to 5 minutes on each side, or until crisp-tender and lightly browned. Transfer from the grill to a large platter and set aside.

When the water is at a full boil, add the fettuccine to the pot, stir it well, and let it cook for 5 to 8 minutes, or until tender but slightly resistant to the bite. While the pasta is cooking, cut the peppers into ¼-inch strips and the squid bodies into ½-inch strips. Heat the remaining 3 tablespoons of olive oil and sauté the garlic for 2 to 3 minutes, or until it is translucent. Stir in the chicken broth and cook over medium heat for about 1 minute. Stir in the peppers, squid, peas, and scallops, and heat through for about 2 minutes. Sprinkle with red pepper flakes, add salt to taste, and stir gently.

Drain the pasta and pour it onto a heated serving platter. Pour the shellfish, vegetables, oil, and garlic over the pasta. Sprinkle with the minced basil and serve at once in flat-rimmed soup bowls.

# GRILLED SNAPPER WITH GRILLED-VEGETABLE SALSA

*Corn-Chili Pudding · Green Salad with Avocado Dressing · Mexican Beer or Sangría*

*Serves 4*

Red snapper is a white-fleshed fish that grills beautifully either whole or filleted. Here it is paired with a simple, colorful salsa made from vegetables cooked briefly on the grill, which brings out their color and flavor while adding the incomparable smoky taste of charcoal. We like to serve this with a green salad with an avocado dressing, and a corn-chili pudding (pureed fresh corn kernels and minced jalapeños cooked in a soufflélike custard). To drink, try Mexican beer or fresh limeade.

**1½ to 2 pounds red snapper fillets**
**2 tablespoons olive oil**
**1 tablespoon red wine vinegar**
**2 tablespoons minced fresh cilantro**
**½ jalapeño chili, seeded and minced**
**Salt to taste**

## Grilled-Vegetable Salsa

**1 yellow bell pepper**
**1 red onion, quartered**
**1 ripe tomato**
**1 or 2 jalapeño chilies**
**1 tablespoon olive oil**
**¼ cup minced fresh cilantro**
**3 tablespoons red wine vinegar**
**Salt to taste**

**Cilantro sprigs for garnish**

Light a charcoal fire in a grill with a hood. While the coals are heating, prepare the fish: Place the fillets in one layer in a shallow nonaluminum container. Combine the oil, vinegar, cilantro, jalapeño, and salt in a small bowl and pour it over the fish. Let the fish sit at room temperature until the coals are hot, about 30 minutes.

When the coals are still flaming and not yet covered with ashes, make the salsa: Place the bell pepper over the flaming coals and cook, turning as necessary, until it is charred on all sides; this will take about 8 minutes. Transfer the pepper to a paper bag, close the bag, and let it sit.

Place the onion, tomato, and jalapeño(s) at the edges of the cooking rack. Cover the grill and cook the vegetables for about 4 minutes. Turn the onion quarters and jalapeño(s); cover the grill and cook for another 4 minutes, or until the tomato is browned and cracked and the onion pieces and jalapeño(s) are tender and browned. Transfer from the grill to a plate and let the vegetables sit at room temperature.

Just before grilling the fish, make the salsa: Rub the charred skin from the peppers and remove the stems and seeds. Split the tomato in half crosswise and hold each half upside down to release some of the seeds. Coarsely chop the pepper, jalapeño(s), onion, and tomato; place in a small bowl. Stir the oil, cilantro, vinegar, and salt to taste into the vegetables; set aside.

When the coals are hot, scrub the hot cooking rack with a grill brush and brush or spray it with oil. Place the fish fillets on the rack and cook them for 2 to 3 minutes on each side, or until the natural divisions of the flesh are just beginning to separate and the fish is opaque throughout. Transfer the fish to a serving plate or plates. Spoon some salsa on each serving of fish and pass the rest alongside; garnish with cilantro and serve at once.

# GRILLED ONO WITH GINGER-GARLIC DIPPING SAUCE

*Grilled Bok Choy Hearts · Grilled Scallop Squash · Sautéed Bok Choy Leaves*
*Steamed Rice · Asian Beer or Gewürztraminer*

*Serves 4*

The ono is a Hawaiian fish with a full flavor and a dense texture that is similar to tuna. Like tuna, it is complemented by assertive tastes such as our ginger-garlic dipping sauce. Serve it with grilled bok choy hearts, grilled scallop squash, and steamed rice. Drink an Asian beer or a spicy wine such as Gewürztraminer with this dish. Tuna steaks may be used in place of the ono fillets in this recipe.

1½ to 2 pounds ono fillets cut ¾ inch thick
2 tablespoons peanut oil
1 tablespoon low-salt soy sauce

## Ginger-Garlic Dipping Sauce

1 tablespoon low-salt soy sauce
2 tablespoons rice vinegar
2 tablespoons water
2 tablespoons grated fresh ginger
2 garlic cloves, minced
½ teaspoon sugar, or to taste

1 large bok choy
6 scallop squash
1 tablespoon peanut oil, plus more for coating
Salt to taste
Cilantro sprigs for garnish

Light a charcoal fire in an open grill. While the coals are heating, place the fish in one layer in a shallow non-aluminum baking dish. Mix together the peanut oil and soy sauce and coat the fish evenly on both sides with the mixture. Let the fish sit at room temperature until the coals are ready, about 30 minutes.

To make the dipping sauce: In a small bowl, combine all the ingredients and set aside at room temperature. Cut the leaves away from the bok choy and set them aside. Cut the white part of the bok choy into 8 lengthwise wedges. Cut the scallops into crosswise slices about ¼ inch thick. Using your hands, coat the vegetables evenly all over with the oil and place them on a plate.

When the coals are hot, place the bok choy and squash on the cooking rack (or use a grill basket) and grill for 5 to 7 minutes on each side, or until browned and tender. Transfer to a plate.

Cut the bok choy leaves into 1-inch-thick shreds. Heat 1 tablespoon of the peanut oil in a large sauté pan or skillet over medium heat, add the bok choy leaves, and cook and stir until the leaves are wilted, about 3 minutes; add salt and set aside.

Scrub the hot cooking rack with a grill brush and spray or brush the rack with oil. Place the fillets over the hot coals and grill them for 3 to 4 minutes on one side. Brush with the marinade left in the marinade pan, turn, and grill for 3 to 4 minutes on the second side, or until the natural divisions of the flesh have just begun to separate and the fish is opaque throughout. Transfer the fish to a heated serving plate or plates and serve with the grilled vegetables, the sautéed bok choy leaves, and individual bowls of dipping sauce. Garnish with cilantro sprigs.

# GRILLED ANGLER WITH ROUILLE AND GRILLED RATATOUILLE

*Orzo · French Bread · Provençal Rosé*

*Serves 4*

A grill meal inspired by the famous Mediterranean dish, bouillabaisse. Serve with orzo (rice-shaped pasta also called *riso* or *puntette*), French bread, and a chilled dry Provençal rosé.

1½ to 2 pounds angler fillets, about ¾ inch thick
2 tablespoons olive oil
1 tablespoon lemon juice
2 tablespoons minced fresh oregano or Italian parsley
Salt to taste

## Rouille

1 red bell pepper
One 1-inch-thick slice French bread (sandwich size)
About ½ cup milk
4 to 6 garlic cloves, smashed
5 tablespoons olive oil
1 tablespoon red wine vinegar
¼ teaspoon cayenne pepper, or to taste
Salt to taste

## Grilled Ratatouille

1 zucchini, halved lengthwise
1 yellow summer squash, halved lengthwise
1 Japanese eggplant, halved lengthwise
1 red bell pepper, stemmed, seeded, and quartered
1 yellow bell pepper, stemmed, seeded, and quartered
1 red onion, quartered
1 basket cherry tomatoes, or about 12 Roma (plum) tomatoes
Olive oil for coating, plus 2 tablespoons
Juice of ½ lemon
2 garlic cloves, minced
2 tablespoons minced fresh oregano or Italian parsley
Salt and freshly ground white pepper to taste

Lemon wedges and oregano or Italian parsley sprigs for garnish

Light a charcoal fire in a grill with a hood, using extra coals. While the coals are heating, prepare the fish: Place the angler fillets in one layer in a shallow nonaluminum container. In a small bowl, combine the olive oil, lemon juice, oregano or parsley, and salt to taste; pour this mixture over the fish, coating both sides evenly. Let the fish sit at room temperature while the coals are heating, about 30 minutes.

While the coals are still flaming and are not yet covered with ash, prepare the rouille: Place the bell pepper on the cooking rack and turn it every few minutes until it is evenly charred on all sides; this will take about 8 minutes. Transfer the pepper from the grill to a paper bag; close the bag and let the pepper sit until it is cool enough to handle, about 15 minutes. Meanwhile, place the bread slice in a shallow bowl and pour the milk over it to soak it evenly.

When the pepper has cooled, rub off most of the charred skin, remove the stem and seeds, and chop the pepper coarsely. Place the pepper in a blender. Squeeze the milk out of the bread slice and tear the bread into chunks, placing them in the blender. Add the remaining rouille ingredients and puree to a smooth sauce. Transfer the sauce to a bowl and adjust the seasoning; the rouille should be quite hot. Set aside at room temperature.

When the coals have stopped flaming but are still very hot, prepare the ratatouille: Cut the zucchini, squash, and eggplant in half down the center so that each is cut into 4 long, thin wedges. Place in a large shallow bowl along with the 2 bell peppers, onion, and tomatoes and, using your hands, coat all the vegetables evenly with olive oil.

Place the vegetables on the cooking rack (use a heated basket or grilling grid if you have one) and cook them for a total of about 6 minutes, turning them 2 or 3 times. Remove the tomatoes, which should be charred and beginning to burst. Cover the grill for 2 or 3 minutes, or until the remaining vegetables are almost tender. Transfer the vegetables, including the tomatoes, to a cutting board and chop them coarsely. Place the chopped vegetables in a large bowl, add the remaining ratatouille ingredients, and adjust the seasoning; set aside at room temperature.

When the coals are hot, scrub the hot cooking rack with a grill brush and spray or brush the rack with oil. Grill the fillets for 3 to 4 minutes on each side, or until the natural divisions of the flesh have just begun to separate and the fish is opaque throughout. Transfer the fish to a serving plate or plates. Serve with a squiggle of rouille on top, accompanied with the ratatouille and garnished with lemon wedges and herb sprigs. Pass the remaining rouille alongside in a bowl.

# GRILLED CATFISH ON A BED OF BRAISED GREENS

*Grilled Cherry Tomatoes · Dirty Rice · Corn Pancakes · Beer or Iced Tea with Mint*

*Serves 4*

Catfish fillets take almost no time to prepare and grill for this satisfying down-home main course. Cajun spice mix, available in a variety of blends, is good on meat and chicken, and is one of the fastest ways to give a special zing to fish. Serve with dirty rice (rice cooked in chicken broth with minced chicken livers, green onions, and green peppers), corn pancakes, and grilled cherry tomatoes. Your favorite local beer is the drink of choice, unless you prefer iced tea with mint.

**1½ pounds catfish fillets**
**1 tablespoon Cajun spice mix**
**¼ cup dry white wine**
**Juice of ½ lemon**
**1 tablespoon peanut oil**
**Salt and freshly ground white pepper to taste**

## Braised Greens

**2 slices bacon, minced**
**3 garlic cloves, minced**
**2 bunches collard greens or Swiss chard, cut into**
**    crosswise shreds**
**¼ cup chicken broth**
**Salt and freshly ground white pepper to taste**

**1 basket cherry tomatoes, stemmed**
**Olive oil for coating**

Prepare a fire in an open charcoal grill. While the coals are heating, prepare the fish: Place the catfish fillets in a shallow nonaluminum container. Combine the Cajun spice mix, wine, lemon juice, oil, and salt and pepper, and pour the mixture over the fish; turn the fish and spread the mixture evenly over the second side. Place 4 wooden skewers in water to cover until time to grill.

Meanwhile, prepare the braised greens: In a large skillet, cook the minced bacon for about 3 minutes, or until it begins to crisp. Add the garlic and cook for another 2 minutes, or until it becomes translucent. Add the shredded greens or chard and chicken broth and sauté until the greens are wilted and the broth has almost evaporated. Season to taste and set aside.

When the coals are hot, coat the tomatoes with olive oil and thread them onto the skewers. Place the tomatoes on the cooking rack and cook them for 3 to 4 minutes on each side, or until slightly wrinkled and browned. Transfer from the grill to a plate.

Scrub the hot cooking rack with a grill brush and spray or brush the rack with oil. Place the fillets perpendicular to the grill grids and cook them for 3 to 4 minutes on each side, or until the natural divisions of the flesh have just begun to separate and the fish is opaque throughout. Transfer from the grill to a plate.

Heat the braised greens for 2 or 3 minutes, or until heated through. Dividing them equally, make a bed of greens on each of 4 hot plates. Divide the fillets equally among the plates, placing them on the braised greens. Push the tomatoes off the skewers and serve them alongside the greens. Serve at once.

# GRILLED TUNA, ARTICHOKE, RADICCHIO, AND FENNEL SALAD

*Hot Orange Scones · White Wine*

*Serves 4*

The subtle flavors of artichoke and fennel, and the slightly bitter taste of radicchio are lovely counterpoints to full-flavored tuna. The vegetables should be grilled ahead and served cooled to room temperature, while the tuna should be hot off the grill, seared on the outside and medium-rare on the inside, if you like. The olive vinaigrette highlights all the flavors of this main-course Mediterranean-inspired salad. Serve it with your favorite white wine and hot orange scones (flavored with fresh orange juice and grated orange zest).

**4 large artichokes**
**1½ pounds tuna fillets, cut ¾ inch thick**
**6 tablespoons oil**
**Juice of 2 lemons**
**2 to 3 tablespoons garlic, minced**
**4 small heads radicchio**
**2 fennel bulbs**
**8 to 10 cups salad greens, preferably a mixture**
  **of red leaf lettuce and mesclun**

## Olive Vinaigrette

**½ cup olive oil**
**1 tablespoon red wine vinegar**
**1 tablespoon fresh lemon juice**
**½ teaspoon olive paste, or**
  **1 teaspoon minced pitted Kalamata olives**

**Kalamata olives for garnish**

Trim the top and bottom of the artichokes and trim each leaf with a pair of scissors. Bring a large pot of salted water to a boil, drop in the artichokes, and cook them until tender, about 30 minutes. Meanwhile, light a charcoal fire in an open grill.

While the coals are heating and the artichokes are cooking, place the tuna in one layer in a shallow non-aluminum container. In a small bowl, mix together the oil, lemon juice, and garlic. Pour half of this mixture over the fish, reserving the remaining half. Let the fish sit at room temperature until the coals are hot, about 30 minutes, turning the fish once or twice.

Remove the artichokes from the water and plunge them into cold water to cool; drain them upside down. Strip off all the leaves and, using a teaspoon, dig out and discard the spiny choke. Cut the radicchio, including the core, into lengthwise quarters. Trim the stems and root end from the fennel and cut the bulb into 8 lengthwise wedges. Coat the artichoke hearts, radicchio, and fennel evenly all over with the remaining oil and lemon mixture.

When the coals are hot, place the vegetables on the grill and cook the artichokes and radicchio for 2 or 3 minutes on each side, or until lightly browned; cook the fennel for 2 or 3 minutes longer on each side, or until browned and tender. Transfer the vegetables to a plate.

Scrub the hot cooking rack with a grill brush and spray or brush the rack with oil. If the coals are not still hot, shake them or push them closer together to make the fire hotter. Place the tuna over the hot coals and cook for 2 to 3 minutes on each side for medium-rare tuna, or 3 to 4 minutes on each side for tuna that is opaque throughout. Transfer the tuna to a plate.

Cut the artichoke hearts crosswise into 3 or 4 slices. Cut the fennel and radicchio wedges crosswise into sections about 2 inches wide, discarding the radicchio cores. Cut the tuna into 1-inch-thick slices. In a small bowl, mix together all the vinaigrette ingredients. Place the salad greens in a large bowl and pour half of the vinaigrette over them; toss gently to coat the greens. Divide the salad greens among 4 large plates and distribute the fish and vegetables over the greens. Pour most of the remaining vinaigrette over the fish and vegetables and pass the rest of the vinaigrette at the table. Garnish with olives and serve.

# EQUIPMENT AND FOOD SOURCES

## Grills

HASTY-BAKE
P.O. Box 471285
Tulsa, OK 74147-1285
800-4AN-OVEN
Charcoal console grills and built-ins.

KAMADO
BSW, Inc.
4680 East Second Street
Benicia, CA 94510
707-745-8175
Ceramic grill-ovens in several sizes.

KINGSFORD COMPANY
P.O. Box 24305
Oakland, CA 94623-9981
800-537-2823
Charcoal kettle grills with shelves, rack, and ash catcher.

THERMOS
Route 75
Freeport, IL 61032
800-435-5194
A wide range of gas console grills with accessories.

WEBER
Weber-Stephen Products Company
560 Hicks Road
Palatine, IL 60067-6971
708-705-8660 (in Illinois) or 800-323-7598;
fax 708-705-7971
Charcoal and gas kettle grills in several sizes and styles; grill accessories.

## Charcoal and Smoking Woods

CHARCOAL COMPANION
7955 Edgewater Drive
Oakland, CA 94621
510-632-2100 (in California) or 800-521-0505;
fax 510-632-1986
A wide variety of smoking woods.

CONNECTICUT CHARCOAL COMPANY
Old Time Charcoal
P.O. Box 742
Westport, CT 06881
203-227-2101
Hardwood charcoal.

DESERT MESQUITE OF ARIZONA
3458 East Illini Street
Phoenix, AZ 85040
602-437-3135
Mesquite smoking woods.

HUMPHREY CHARCOAL CORPORATION
P.O. Box 440
Brookville, PA 15825
814-849-2302
Wholesale and regional only; call for names of distributors of hardwood lump charcoal and hardwood charcoal briquettes.

LAZZARI FUEL COMPANY
P.O. Box 34051
San Francisco, CA 94134
415-467-2970 (in California) or 800-242-7265
Mesquite charcoal and smoking woods.

LUHR JENSEN & SONS, INC.
P.O. Box 297
Hood River, OR 97031
503-386-3811 (in Oregon) or 800-535-1711
Smoking woods.

## Grilling Accessories

CHARCOAL COMPANION
7955 Edgewater Drive
Oakland, CA 94621
510-632-2100 (in California) or 800-521-0505;
fax 510-632-1986
A wide variety of grill accessories.

GRIFFO PRODUCTS
1400 North 30th Street
Quincy, IL 62301
217-222-0700
Grilling grids and grill baskets.

OUTDOOR COMPANY (O.D.C.)
P.O. Box 6255
Evansville, IN 47719-0255
800-544-5362
Accessories and replacement parts for gas grills.

WEBER
Weber-Stephen Products Company
560 Hicks Road
Palatine, IL 60067-6971
708-705-8660 (in Illinois) or 800-446-1070;
fax 708-705-7971
Accessories for kettle grills; grilling tools.

## Fish and Shellfish

SIMPLY SHRIMP
7794 NW 44th Street
Ft. Lauderdale, FL 33351
800-833-0888
Gulf shrimp, tuna, Florida pompano, yellowtail, and a wide variety of other fresh fish and shellfish in season.

JAKE'S FAMOUS PRODUCTS
4252 SE International Way, Suite G
Milwaukie, OR 97222
503-226-1420
Northwest salmon, Dungeness crab, oysters, crawfish, and other fresh fish and shellfish in season.

S. T. MOORE SEAFOOD
Route 2, P.O. Box 33
Hebron, MD 21830
800-325-CRAB
Live blue crabs, Atlantic lobsters, and oysters; trout, bluefish, angler, and other fresh fish and shellfish in season.

# BIBLIOGRAPHY

Cronin, Isaac; Harlow, Jay; and Johnson, Paul. *The California Seafood Cookbook*. Berkeley, Ca.: Aris Books, 1983.

The Editors of Time-Life Books. *Fish*. Alexandria, Va.: Time-Life Books, 1979.

——. *Outdoor Cooking*. Alexandria, Va.: Time-Life Books, 1983.

McCune, Kelly. *The Fish Book*. New York: Harper & Row, 1988.

*Simply Seafood: America's Seafood Magazine*. Summer 1992.

Sinnes, A. Cort. *The Grilling Encyclopedia*. New York: Atlantic Monthly Press, 1992.

## GRILL BOOK
*Recipes*

**Butterflied Leg of Lamb with Zinfandel Sauce**

**Veal Chops with Gruyère and Prosciutto**

**Skewered Scallops, Zucchini, and Artichoke Hearts with Salsa**

**Grilled Whole Trout**

**Grilled Steak with Fresh Herbs**

**Salmon Steaks with Chive Butter**

**Tofu Marinated in Sesame Oil and Rice Vinegar with Scallions**

**Rock Cornish Game Hens in Raspberry Vinegar Marinade**

**Sesame Flank Steak**

**Boneless Pork Loin in Sherry Vinegar, Port, and Prune Marinade**

**Grilled Split Lobster Tail**

**Mixed Sausage Grill**

**Chicken Breasts in Many Mustards**

**Nam Prik Shrimp**

**Grilled Breast of Duck in Red Wine Marinade**

**Peanut Chicken on Skewers**

**Barbecued Baby Back Pork Ribs in Honey, Tamari, and Orange Marinade**

**Grill Appetizer Party**

## THE ART OF GRILLING
*Recipes*

Grilled Italian Appetizers

Tandoori Chicken

Rack of Lamb with Port, Rosemary, and Garlic Marinade

Soft-Shell Crab with Hazelnut Butter

Burgers and Red Onion Slices

Boneless Quail with Corn Bread and Escarole Stuffing

Peppers Stuffed with Eggplant

Prawns with Spicy Remoulade

Tenderloin of Beef with Mustard-Mint Sauce

Calves' Liver with Sage Butter and Pancetta

Lime-marinated Rock Cornish Game Hens

Ham Steak with Apple Cream Sauce

Grapevine-smoked Salmon, Trout, and Oysters

Veal Roast with Marsala and Dried Apricots

Hickory-grilled Pork Chops with Fresh Peaches

Rabbit with Pecan Butter and Apples

Monkfish with Caper Vinaigrette

Steak Teriyaki Rice Bowl

Thai Barbecued Chicken

Spiedini with Balsamic Marinade

Swordfish with Pico de Gallo

Turkey Breast Smoked with Cherry Wood

Sea Bass on Bok Choy with Ginger-Garlic Butter

Hickory-smoked Country-style Ribs with Barbecue Sauce

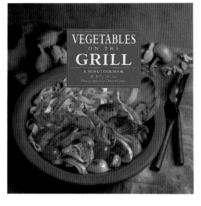

## VEGETABLES ON THE GRILL
*Recipes*

Polenta with Green Chili and Red Pepper

Coconut, Lime, and Ginger–marinated Vegetables

Roasted Acorn Squash with Wild Rice Salad

Sandwich Grill

Skewered Vegetables with Cilantro Sauce

Yams, Apples, and Leeks with Spicy Pecan Nut Butter

Fresh Figs and Vegetables with Couscous

Baby Vegetables with Pasta and Fresh Herb Sauce

Root Vegetables with Warm Mustard Greens Sauce

Skewered Tofu, Mushrooms, Daikon, and Bok Choy with a Soy, Ginger, and Orange Marinade

Grilled Appetizers

Corn Bread–stuffed Peppers with Chipotle Sauce

Middle Eastern Eggplant Sandwich with Tahini Dressing

Vegetable Medley with Three Dipping Sauces

Summer Salad with Quinoa

Corn Cakes with Roasted Vegetables

Vegetables with Northern Indian Almond-Spice Sauce

Garlicky Portobello Mushrooms

Basil and Pine Nut Polenta

Grilled Tempeh with Red Onion and Eggplant on Whole-Wheat Toast

Eggplant, New Potato, and Fennel with Sour Cream Sauce

Tofu Satay with Tangy Dipping Sauce

Grill Cocktail Party

Wood-smoked Pizzas

## CHICKEN ON THE GRILL
*Recipes*

Tom's Asian-style Drumettes

Grilled Chicken Breasts with Whole-Grain Mustard Sauce

Whole Grill-roasted Chicken Stuffed with Wild Rice and Shiitake Mushrooms

Grilled Chicken Breasts with Apricot, Raisin, and Marsala Sauce

Mesquite-smoked Chicken Breasts with Grilled Poblano-Tomatillo Sauce

Grilled Caribbean Chicken

Vine-smoked Chicken Breasts with Herbs and Mustard-Cream Sauce

Grill-roasted Chicken with Corn Bread Stuffing

Grilled Quail with Leeks

Hot Fourth-of-July Barbecued Chicken

Thai-style Grilled Poussins with Peanut Sauce

Chicken Fajitas

Grilled Mediterranean Chicken

Tandoori Chicken Kabobs

Hickory-smoked Whole Chicken with Kansas City Barbecue Sauce

Grilled Boned Turkey Breast Stuffed with Emmenthaler Cheese and Prosciutto

Grilled Pheasant with a Sauce of Shiitake Mushrooms, Cream, and Brandy

Smoked Sesame Chicken on a Bed of Bitter Greens

Cajun-style Grilled Chicken

Chinese Barbecued Chicken

Grilled Breaded Chicken Thighs

Grilled Port-marinated Chicken with Prunes

Grilled Chicken Breasts in Yellow Curry with Fresh Nectarine Chutney

Grilled Cornish Hens with Chili Butter and Grilled-Corn Salsa

Twice-grilled Duck Breast in a Raspberry Vinegar Marinade

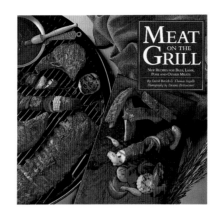

## MEAT ON THE GRILL
*Recipes*

New York Steak with Brandy and Black Pepper Sauce

Porterhouse Steak with a Sauce of Shallots and Jim Beam

Grilled Tenderloin of Beef with Fresh Horseradish and Watercress Sauces

Grilled Marinated Flank Steak with Sweet-Pepper Relish

Alder-smoked Brisket with Chili Paste and Smoked-Tomato Salsa

Beef Satay with Japanese Eggplant and Peanut Sauce

Korean Barbecued Beef with Grilled Baby Leeks and Ginger Dipping Sauce

Steak Fajitas with Grilled-Papaya Salsa

Variations on the Perfect Hamburger

Rack of Lamb Marinated in Pomegranate Juice and Served with Fresh-Mint Sauce

Olive wood–smoked Saddle of Lamb with Olive Paste and and Aïoli

Grilled Butterflied Leg of Lamb with Indian Spices and Cucumber Chutney

Lamb Kabobs with Summer Vegetables, Bay Leaves, and Garlic-Yogurt Sauce

Grilled Pork Chops with Fresh Tomato-Pepper Relish

Grilled Pork Tenderloins with Apple-Sherry Sauce

Grilled Pork Loin with Warm Dried-Fruit Compote

Crown Roast of Pork with a Sauce of Cherries, Cream, and Port, Stuffed with Wild Rice

Pork Kabobs with Apples, Fennel, Red Onion, Figs, and Sage Vinaigrette

Hickory-smoked Baby Back Ribs

Pork Spareribs in a Hot Bean Paste Marinade

Vine-smoked Rabbit with a Sauce of Red Wine and Fresh Herbs

Grilled Veal Chops with Fresh Oregano

Grilled Veal Rolls with Fresh Tomato-Basil Sauce

Grilled Veal Roast with Sage-Hazelnut Butter

Grilled Loin of Venison with Fresh Cranberry-Chili Chutney

# INDEX

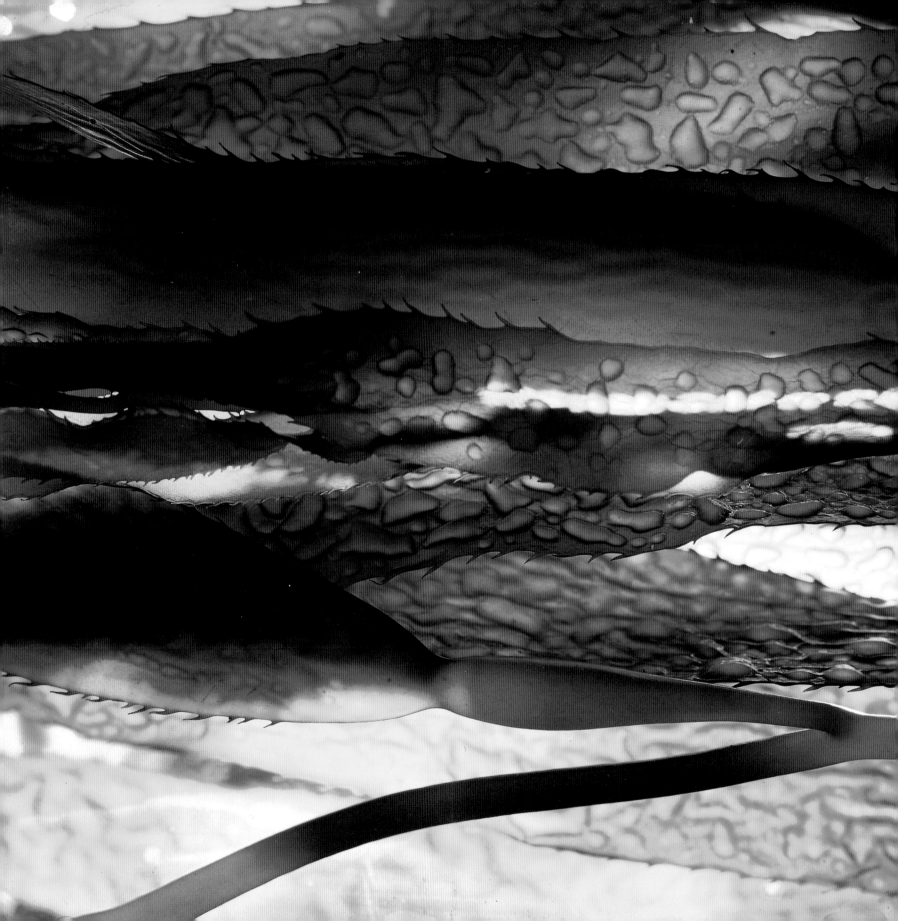